Tropical Fish

Brian Ward

Macdonald Guidelines

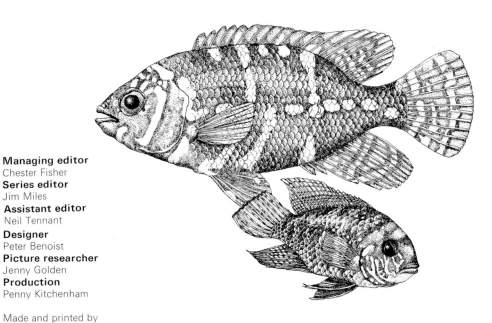

Managing editor
Chester Fisher
Series editor
Jim Miles
Assistant editor
Neil Tennant
Designer
Peter Benoist
Picture researcher
Jenny Golden
Production
Penny Kitchenham

Made and printed by
Waterlow (Dunstable) Limited

ISBN 0 356 06027 6

Contents

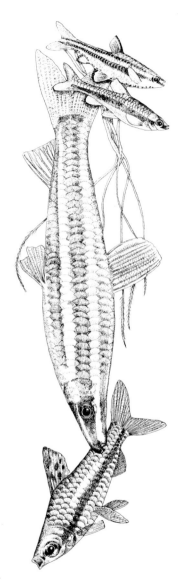

Information

Activities

Reference

©Copyright Macdonald Educational 1978
First published 1978
Macdonald Educational Ltd
Holywell House, Worship Street,
London EC2A 2EN

Fish keeping

Why keep tropical fish as pets? Surely they are expensive, delicate, and difficult to maintain in a healthy and attractive condition? This is a common reaction of many of the people who gaze, fascinated, into a tank of brightly coloured fish. At some time or other, almost all of us have kept fish; usually goldfish who peer hopelessly through dirty and discoloured tanks or bowls for a short while before their premature deaths. Don't let experiences of this sort put you off from one of the easiest and most rewarding hobbies. Goldfish are actually rather difficult to keep in the home. The water gets too warm, and because of their messy feeding habits, soon becomes polluted and foul unless scrupulous care is taken.

With the modern tropical fish tank, we are talking about a tiny self-contained world, in which you control everything yourself; the seasons, length of daylight, population size, climate, and food supply. All very complicated? Not a bit of it. Looking after tropical fish takes only a few minutes of your time each day, unless you wish to keep some of the more exotic and specialized types.

Beauty and behaviour

You will probably find that you actually spend a lot of your time just looking at your fish, and that is why you keep them in the first place. You will soon find that there is a lot more to fish than a mere decorative tank of jewel-like creatures adorning a corner of your living room. Like other animals, fish have a huge range of complicated and fascinating behaviour patterns which you can observe in your own home.

For example, you might keep fish which jump out of the water to lay their eggs on overhanging leaves. Or one which can shoot down flies with a well-aimed drop of water.

If you are solely interested in the beauty of your fish, you have a choice of all the colours of the rainbow, and an infinite variety of shapes and sizes.

But what you must realize is that all these types of fish have special requirements of some sort. After all, they come from countries all around the world, living originally in habitats ranging from puddles, to lakes, rivers, and mountain streams, so it is hardly reasonable to expect all these varied types to thrive in one small tank. This book attempts to explain not only the broad principles of tropical fish-keeping, but also how the original habitats and natural behaviour of fish affect their suitability for keeping in the home aquarium.

The correct conditions

There are some fish so hardy, and with such peaceful natures, that they can be kept by the least expert aquarist with very little attention. These are the common Guppies, Swordtails, Barbs, and so on which can be seen in almost every pet shop, and which have been kept in aquaria for many years. But if you restrict yourself to these 'safe' types, and don't bother to learn

▶ The well-designed tropical aquarium contains a careful blend of plants and rockwork, setting off the colours and shapes of the fish themselves. Properly cared for, the tank will maintain itself for years with the minimum of attention.

a little more about fish habits and requirements, you will be missing out on some of the most interesting types.

Similarly, if you simply dump a few large rocks and one or two plastic plants in your tank, you will be missing the beauty of the best aquarium plants, which can make your tank look more attractive, make it a better home for your fish, and even make it easier to maintain in a healthy condition.

If you get all the conditions right (and once you have grasped the general principles it is very easy to do so), your aquarium should look after itself with only the minimum of attention. Just add the correct amount of food, switch the tank lights on and off at the right times, and add a little fresh water occasionally, and that's about it, other than a small amount of cleaning and tidying up. Even holidays are no problem, as your fish can go without any food at all for quite a while without coming to any harm.

The aquarium can look after itself because it is truly a small world of its own. It is almost self-contained; 'almost' because you must still supply some of the essentials needed to keep your aquarium world running smoothly. Most of the fish come from the tropics, so it is essential to heat the tank in some way. Even in centrally-heated homes conditions are not continuously warm enough for healthy fish. It only takes an overnight temperature drop to chill them, and make them liable to disease. So the tropical tank is always heated, and normally uses the simplest possible electric heater, sealed in a glass tube. To control the temperature accurately, a thermostat is used to switch the heater on and off. This can be either submerged in the tank, stuck on the glass, or combined with the heater in one unit. To keep an accurate check on the temperature, and to avoid expensive accidents, a thermometer must be used.

(Most tropical fish thrive at temperatures between 25–27°C.) You will obviously need a suitable tank; these and other items of essential equipment are discussed in detail in the next section of this book. Many other gadgets are available, but only a few more are strictly necessary. Lighting is normally built into the cover of the tank, and a pump delivering air to the tank itself or to a filter is extremely useful.

Cleaning by 'recycling'

So having set it all up, with the proper types of fish and plants, how does it all work, and why does the aquarium stay so much cleaner than the traditional goldfish globe? Our aquarium uses the modern ecological concept of 'recycling'. Broadly speaking, this means that the fish produce waste, which is broken down by naturally occuring bacteria in the gravel, and the resulting chemicals are consumed by the plants, making any poisonous waste inactive. You can help the process along by including fish like Catfish which clean up odd pieces of uneaten food, and even graze on decaying plant leaves. All you have to add is food for the fish, warmth for both fish and plants, and lights to allow the plants to grow well. You also have to remove any large particles of dirt, and clean the glass of any micro-organisms that might obscure your view of the fish.

Which fish?

The question of which fish and plants to keep in your tank is a matter of personal preference. Many types are listed in this book, together with some of their most important features which should help you in making your selection. You will also find that the correct scientific names for fish and plants are used. This is to avoid confusion. There are literally thousands of species of fish kept in aquaria, and in most cases the popular names bestowed on them by the importers or the pet trade are meaningless and confusing. There are exceptions, of course. Everyone can recognize a Guppy, Angelfish, Discus, and so on, but a Headstander could be any one of a dozen or more fish. The scientific name is in two parts. First the generic name, followed by the species, such as *Brachydanio rerio*, the common Zebra Fish. Other related species are *B. albolineatus, B. nigrofasciatus*, and so on. (The generic name is shortened to an initial letter after the first mention.) To those with a smattering of Latin, these names give a clue to the characteristics of the fish. *Albolineatus* implies a pearly line, and *nigrofasciatus* means that the fish has dark speckles, although sometimes the names can be quite arbitrary. Unfortunately, the scientists responsible for naming fish quite often have second thoughts and change a well-established name. Although the correct names are used throughout this book where possible, in some cases it would be perverse to refer to a fish by a new and unrecognizable name, when it has been known by another for many years. Where this happens, alternative names are given in brackets.

▼ Fluorescent tubes (1) are ideal for the home aquarium, providing adequate light with a minimum of excess heat.

▼ Thermometers (2, 3) are essential, keeping an accurate check on the working of heaters and thermostats.

▼ Use combined heater/ thermostats (4) in the smaller tank, but separate units in the larger aquarium.

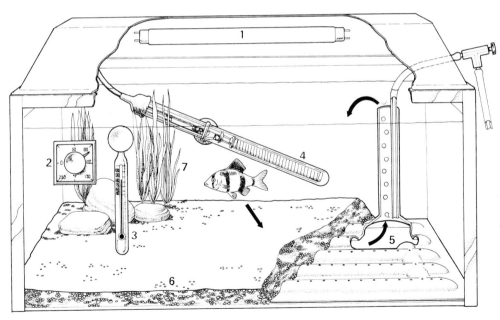

▲ The air lift, powered by a stream of air from a simple electric pump, operates the filters (5) which dispose of fish droppings and uneaten food. Gravel (6) has the dual function of decoration and providing a growing medium for plants (7). It can also form a part of the tank filtration system.

The fish's needs

Living in a tiny, enclosed environment, pet fish are entirely dependent on their owners for their welfare. You control their world entirely, and unless you get the conditions right, you will have only limited success with your fish.

Your fish exist in water which comes straight from the tap, but just consider where they, or their ancestors, originally lived. Not in sparkling clear and purified tap water, with a trace of chlorine to kill off most of the germs, and perhaps with added fluoride to improve dental health. They probably originated in a large, slow-moving river in South America or South-East Asia, thick with mud and suspended leaves, and rich in micro-organisms. Some may have come from lakes; others would have lived in rain puddles which dried up for most of the year. Others again come from brackish mangrove swamps, where they live in muddy, half-saline water. Marine fish have a different set of requirements. Obviously sea water is much the same everywhere, but the habitat varies between open sea and shallow coral reefs.

What all these habitats have in common is oxygen, dissolved in the water and breathed in by the fish through its gills.

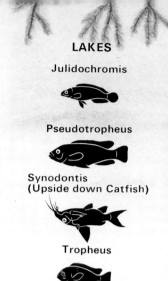

LAKES

Julidochromis

Pseudotropheus

Synodontis
(Upside down Catfish)

Tropheus

ANNUAL PUDDLES

Aphyosemion

Nothobranchius

SWAMPS

Betta

Colisa

Macropodus

RIVERS

Barbus arulius

Botia
(Clown loach)

Cardinal tetra

Corydoras

Hyphessobrycon

Labeo

Pterophyllum

STREAMS

Epalzeorhynchus

Synnocheilus

Tanichthys

BRACKISH WATER

Chanda

Monodactylus

Poeciliidae

Scatophagus

Telmatherina

Tetraodon

SEA

Amphiprion

Balistoides

Chaetodon

Dascyllus

Platax

Pomocanthus

Pterois

How fish breathe

The contact between water and air provides oxygen, the greatest need of all fish. As oxygen is dissolved at the surface, this means that rapidly moving or circulating water, such as a mountain stream, contains most oxygen, while a stagnant pool may contain very little. Certain fish, such as trout, can only live in high-oxygen conditions, so trout and other mountain-stream fish are generally difficult to keep in the aquarium without constant running water. On the other hand, fish living in small pools or swamps are accustomed not only to lack of oxygen, but also to sudden changes in water conditions when it rains. Such fish make the hardiest inhabitants of the aquarium. Some, known generally as Labyrinth Fish, have even developed special organs to allow them to breathe air direct from the surface, making them almost independent of dissolved oxygen. The familiar Siamese Fighter, *Betta splendens*, is one such air-breather.

Like all other air-breathing animals, fish breathe out carbon dioxide, a gas which, like oxygen, is dissolved in the water. It leaves the water at the surface, passing out into the air. In stagnant water, particularly if fish are overcrowded, this waste gas builds up in the water until the fish become quite literally suffocated. When this happens you will see them 'gasping' at the surface, in obvious distress. This is where the aquarium aerator or air pump comes in. Its flow of bubbles circulates the water, allowing carbon dioxide to leave, and fresh oxygen to be dissolved.

The tank environment

In natural conditions, plants play an essential part in this continuous recycling. All freshwater fish habitats have some plant life. As part of the plant's normal life process, it takes in carbon dioxide during the daylight hours, and gives off oxygen, which the fish can use. You can often see tiny bubbles of oxygen on the surface of the leaves in a well-planted aquarium. At night the process is reversed; the plant absorbs oxygen and gives off carbon dioxide. Unless something has gone badly wrong with the conditions in the aquarium, this will not bother the fish. Most of them remain inactive at night to avoid over-use of the depleted oxygen, if they normally come from stagnant waters. River fish, however, would not normally notice the difference, and often continue to forage at night. Once more, you can easily override this variation in dissolved gas content of the aquarium water by use of the aerator.

Carbon dioxide is not the only waste product produced by the fish. Their excrement and uneaten food also contribute to the chemical balance of the water. Fish also produce urine, which is less apparent but equally significant. All these waste materials are acted on by the teeming hordes of bacteria present in the established aquarium. Their presence is not an indication of unhygienic conditions; on the contrary, without them the aquarium will not remain healthy for very long. All these waste products, and particularly urea in the fish urine, are broken down by bacterial action to simpler and less toxic chemicals. These consist largely of nitrates and nitrites, which are essential ingredients of garden fertilizers. In the aquarium too they are used by the plants, so in this way the fish and plant population balance each other's needs. But if the fish population is too large, the plants may not be able to dispose of all the waste, and nitrate and nitrite levels will increase to a poisonous level. Like other types of plants, aquatic plants have growing seasons, so what was a healthy tank during seasons when the tank lighting was augmented by natural sunlight may suddenly become a poisonous trap for the fish when growth stops during the shorter winter days. Some of the means of avoiding this problem, like periodic water changes or special filters, are discussed in the next section of this book.

The chemical content of water

Other essential parts of the habitat are water hardness, and pH, or alkalinity/acidity. Hardness or DH, and pH are often confused. DH is a measure of the amount of the chemicals calcium and magnesium dissolved in the water, and this is determined by the original source of the water. Generally speaking, very hard tap water comes from limestone or chalk areas, while soft water, without these dissolved chemicals, comes from granite areas. pH measures acidity, and in practice soft water is generally acidic, with a low pH value, while hard water is often alkaline. This is by no means certain, however, and if in doubt you must check with your local water company or a knowledgeable aquarist before buying fish known to be sensitive to these factors.

Other dissolved materials have a similar impact on the environment. Peat, for example, adds a number of organic chemicals to the water, which are essential for the health of some fish.

So your fish may, although it is unlikely, come from a mountain stream in the tropics with relatively cool water, rich in oxygen and containing very little carbon dioxide. Probably it will be very hard water with a high level of dissolved solids.

Let us compare this with a fish living in a small pool deep in a tropical rain forest. The water is stagnant and deficient in oxygen because of the lack of current, while relatively high in carbon dioxide. The pool is warmer and fed by very soft rainwater. It will be rich in chemical foods because of the quantity of decaying vegetation it contains, and so huge numbers of micro-organisms will be present—a plentiful food source able to feed the large fish population. The conditions in this small, enclosed environment are much closer to the aquarium than the stream or river, and, because of the violent changes in water characteristics after heavy rain and at different seasons, the fish will be hardy.

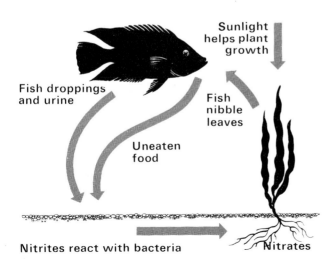

Sunlight helps plant growth

Fish droppings and urine

Fish nibble leaves

Uneaten food

Nitrites react with bacteria

Nitrates

◄ Organic decay in the aquarium results from the attacks of bacteria on uneaten food, fish droppings and dead parts of plants, liberating substances rich in nitrogen. To this is added the large amount of nitrogen present in fish urine. Bacteria act on these substances to produce highly toxic nitrites which in turn react with other bacteria to produce the less poisonous nitrates. These are used by the plants as a growth chemical, completing the nitrogen cycle.

Types of fish

Fish are probably the most diverse of all vertebrates, or animals with backbones. As we have seen, they inhabit an enormous range of different aquatic environments, and are extensively modified for this purpose. These modifications, such as fantastic body shapes or beautiful colours, are what make them suitable for the aquarium. The diagram to the right shows the general structure of an 'average' fish, although strictly speaking there is no such thing as 'average'. Every single fish is modified for some special purpose.

Starting with basic, spindle-shaped fish —probably the ancestral type—we can now see how they have become modified to suit their habitat. The Salmonid or salmon-like fish are adapted for rapid swimming. Among tropical aquarium fish we can see several types having similar shapes, and sharing the same habit of powerful swimming. Quite often, this torpedo-shaped body is equipped with a streamlined and deeply-forked tail, like that of the Tunny, which makes for even faster swimming and also for powerful leaping. So there are a whole range of distantly related fish, sharing the same body shape, and having much the same habits. Typical examples of this type would be the freshwater 'sharks' from South East Asia and Africa, *Labeo* species (actually quite unrelated to sharks), *Hemiodus* from the Amazon region, and *Anostomus, Leporinus*, and *Chilodus* from the same area. With a little practice, it is possible to tell a lot about the probable behaviour of a fish just from its shape. Flattened and streamlined fish are usually modified to withstand the force of river currents; fish with barbels or whiskers around their mouths will prob-

ably spend most of their time grubbing about the bottom of the tank, looking for food. Many fish have a straight upper surface to their bodies. This is an adaptation to allow them to feed near the surface, without actually breaking the surface with their backs. Still others, like the Cichlids, are relatively slow-moving, yet have powerful bodies, large fins, and predatory jaws. They are best suited to making short but very fast dashes after their prey.

Even within each of the large families of fish, some of which are described below, there is enormous variation. Each of the families has some members adapted to life in almost every freshwater aquatic habitat.

Cyprinids

The largest of all the families of freshwater fish is the *Cyprinidae*; the family containing the carp and minnows of the rivers in cooler climates. In the aquarium, this group is represented principally by the Barbs and the Rasboras. They occur widely around the world, being absent only from South America, Australasia, Madagascar, and the colder areas.

The Cyprinids are often very large fish. Some may be two metres or more in length, but as they are such a huge family, there are many smaller types suitable for the aquarium. They generally have an elongated body, with small fins, and a well-forked tail, and often have barbels around the mouth. They do not have normal teeth, instead gulping their food, and grinding it against horny pads in the

throat. Their scales are very large and reflect light well in a series of sparkling highlights—part of the reason for their attraction to the aquarist. As would be expected from their shape and appearance, most of them are powerful, restless swimmers, and so require a good deal of tank space. Probably due to their restless nature, many of the larger Cyprinids are rather aggressive, tending to nip the flowing fins of smaller species, and to keep them away from food.

The smaller and more peaceful types, such as the small Barbs, Rasboras, and Danios, are so hardy and easy to care for that they have become 'standard' fish for the aquarist, being especially suited to the community tank.

▲ Almost every fish is built to the same basic plan, with the dorsal fin (1) and anal fin (2) serving to steady the body in the water, and to prevent rolling. The caudal fin or tail (3) is generally responsible for propulsion, aided by the pectoral fins (4) which are also used for steering. Ventral or pelvic fins (5) work like the elevators of an aircraft, while the lateral line (6) is a sensor which helps the fish to navigate. Even in fish of such diverse shapes as the Angelfish and the Coolie Loach, these basic characteristics still exist.

Most aquarium Cyprinids are omnivorous, feeding on almost anything which is offered, but a few are completely vegetarian, and need special care.

Characins

The other major group is the family of Characins, which come mostly from South and Central America. Many also occur in Africa, but these have not yet become popular as aquarium fish. They are superficially quite similar to the Cyprinids, but differ in several important ways. One is that they possess teeth, which are often well developed, and used to good effect, as in the notorious Piranha. In the smaller types the teeth are not apparent, and a surer guide to the family ancestry is the presence of the small adipose fin, situated between the dorsal fin and the tail. This adipose fin is almost always present in true Characins, but is also often present in catfish. Most Characins are brightly coloured, peaceable, shoaling fish, and the Tetras are the group most widely kept in the aquarium. Most prefer very soft water, which

is in any case necessary for successful breeding. The more popular types will tolerate ordinary tap water, however.

The shape and behaviour of Characins is also more diverse than that of the Cyprinids. Some are cylindrically bodied, powerful swimmers and prodigious leapers, like *Hemiodus* and *Anostomus*. Others are flattened and disc-like, as are the Silver Dollars like *Metynnis* and its close relatives. Their fins tend to be small and neat, but in some types, like the Bleeding Heart Tetra *Hyphessobrycon rubrostigma*, the dorsal and anal fins have long decorative streamers. This group also contains the most brilliantly coloured of all freshwater fish, like the Neon Tetra *H. innesi,* and its relative the Cardinal Tetra *Cheirodon axelrodi*.

Most Characins are omnivorous and easily fed in the aquarium, with dried food and occasional additional live food. Some, like *Metynnis*, need a vegetarian diet, while others are exclusively carnivorous. A few are very pike-like in appearance and habit, and so are unsuited to all but the specialist

CYPRINIDS

CHARACINS

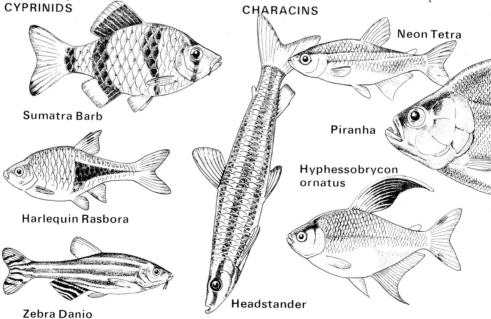

Sumatra Barb

Harlequin Rasbora

Zebra Danio

Neon Tetra

Piranha

Hyphessobrycon ornatus

Headstander

aquarist. Most are eminently suited to the home aquarium, however, and it has been estimated that 60 per cent of all fish bred for the aquarium are Characins.

Egglaying Tooth Carps

This confusing name distinguishes a large group of tropical freshwater fish from their close relatives, the livebearers, which are also part of the same family of Cyprinodonts. Fortunately this group are also known by the more convenient name of Killifish.

The Killifish are found over most of the tropical world, apart from Australasia. They are all small, brightly coloured fish with long trailing dorsal, anal, and caudal fins, and are generally pike-shaped. That is to say, they are elongated, adapted in shape to lying just below the water surface in wait for prey, and are usually carnivorous, having large mouths and sharp teeth

Almost all the Killifish come from stagnant or slow-flowing waters, and a few even live in seasonal rain puddles, which are dry for most of the year. These are known as annual fish, and they survive by laying their eggs deep in the mud, dying as the pool dries out later in the year, but having ensured the survival of the next generation by means of the drought-resistant eggs which will hatch after the next season's rain.

These incredibly beautiful but short-lived Killifish can be kept in very small tanks; some of the annual types will even spawn when kept in a jam jar! They are not suitable for a community tank, however, as most are very aggressive. Killifish are probably best left to the specialist, as they demand very soft water, specialized breeding techniques, and live foods.

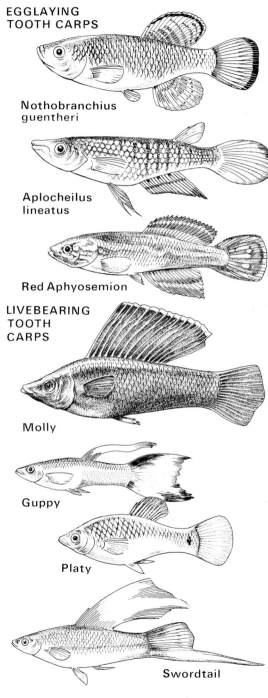

EGGLAYING TOOTH CARPS

Nothobranchius guentheri

Aplocheilus lineatus

Red Aphyosemion

LIVEBEARING TOOTH CARPS

Molly

Guppy

Platy

Swordtail

Livebearing Tooth Carps

Guppies, Swordtails, Mollies, and Platies are among the most familiar of all aquarium fish. Like the former group, they are Cyprinidonts, but they vary in that they produce live young, so they are known colloquially as livebearers. All the true livebearers come from the New World, and the most popular types originated in Central America. They inhabit similar slow-moving or stagnant water to their egglaying relatives, but do not have the ability to survive through drought. The livebearers we now see in the aquarium bear little resemblance to their drab ancestors. They are so easy to breed, and so prolific that it has been possible to breed new colour variations and fish with entirely new fin shapes. The Black Mollie is the best known of these. Other new variants have arisen because it has been possible to cross individuals from different genera, such as Platies and Swordtails, to produce Swordtailed Platies with absolutely no parallel in nature.

Most livebearers live in hard-water regions, and also prefer water with a high pH value; i.e., alkaline conditions. Some even live in the sea for part of their lives, especially the spectacular Sailfin Mollies, *Poecilia velifera* and *latipinna*. Mollies in particular are largely vegetarian, and need green food in their diet if they are to remain healthy. Most other livebearers exist happily in the aquarium on a diet of dried food, occasionally supplemented with live food. One very specialized type, *Belonesox belizanus*, is exclusively carnivorous, and resembles a small pike in appearance and habits. It is too big and too specialized for the average aquarist, who is usually content with the more common livebearers, ranging from 2-10cm.

Cichlids

Throughout South America, Africa, and parts of India the perch-like Cichlid family is found. All are powerfully built fish with strong jaws, and heavily spined dorsal fins. Most are carnivorous, but a few species graze on algae. They are adapted to live in almost every freshwater habitat, but most are far too pugnacious for the community aquarium, with the exception of some old favourites like the Angel Fish, *Pterophyllum scalare*. Some dwarf types are especially suited to the home aquarium, while others like the Discus, *Symphysodon*, are among the most expensive and delicate fish kept by the aquarist. Many of the larger Cichlids dig up all the plants in the tank, and are too aggressive to be kept with other fish.

CICHLIDS

Angelfish

Firemouth Cichlid

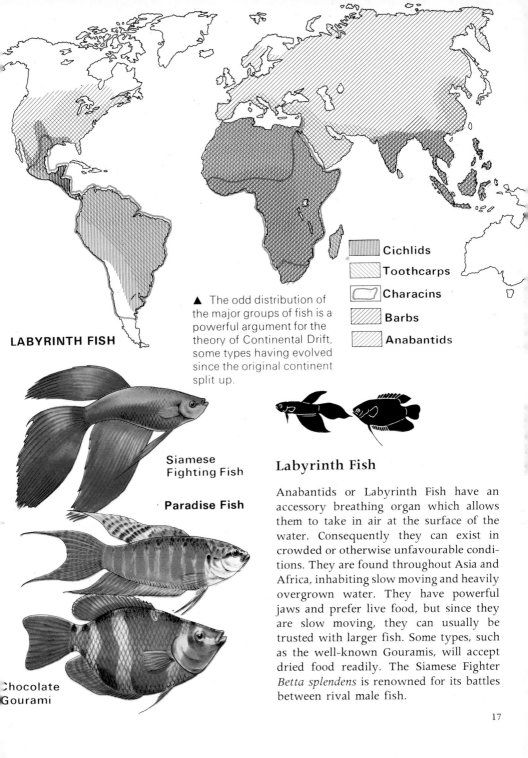

▲ The odd distribution of the major groups of fish is a powerful argument for the theory of Continental Drift, some types having evolved since the original continent split up.

Cichlids
Toothcarps
Characins
Barbs
Anabantids

LABYRINTH FISH

Siamese
Fighting Fish

Paradise Fish

Chocolate
Gourami

Labyrinth Fish

Anabantids or Labyrinth Fish have an accessory breathing organ which allows them to take in air at the surface of the water. Consequently they can exist in crowded or otherwise unfavourable conditions. They are found throughout Asia and Africa, inhabiting slow moving and heavily overgrown water. They have powerful jaws and prefer live food, but since they are slow moving, they can usually be trusted with larger fish. Some types, such as the well-known Gouramis, will accept dried food readily. The Siamese Fighter *Betta splendens* is renowned for its battles between rival male fish.

17

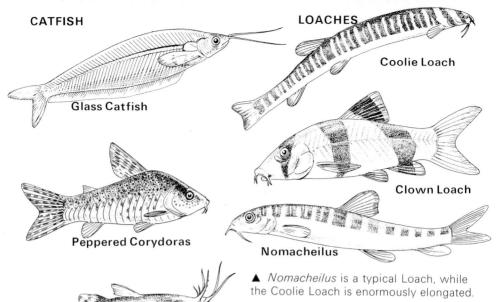

CATFISH

Glass Catfish

Peppered Corydoras

Upside-Down Catfish

LOACHES

Coolie Loach

Clown Loach

Nomacheilus

▲ *Nomacheilus* is a typical Loach, while the Coolie Loach is enormously elongated.

▲ Even within a single group like the Catfish, an enormous range of shapes and markings exists.

Catfish

Catfish are found in all tropical freshwaters except Australasia, and many also live in more temperate areas. They all have barbels around the mouth with which they seek out food. Most have an adipose fin. Their bodies are either naked, or covered with armoured plates; none have normal scales. Most catfish are nocturnal, and physically adapted to life on the bottom, but a few are voracious predators. They come from all types of aquatic environment, and there are hundreds of species suitable for the aquarium. Catfish are very useful inhabi-

tants of the home aquarium, scavenging for uneaten particles of food. Some types have sucker mouths, with which they clean algae from the glass and plants.

Loaches

The loaches are elongated, bottom-living fish with barbels around their mouths. They have smooth, apparently scaleless skins, and are armed with a large spine beneath each eye, which they use for defence. Loaches are found throughout Europe and Asia, but those kept in the aquarium come from South-East Asia. They have an odd habit of dashing suddenly to the surface, and swallowing a bubble of air. This is then absorbed through the wall of their gut, supplementing the oxygen they breathe through their gills. In the aquarium, they behave like the more peaceable catfish, being largely nocturnal, and industrious scavengers.

How fish reproduce

As you might expect from their diverse shapes and habits, the breeding behaviour of fish is extremely varied. The colour of fish is always seen at its best during breeding, and the behaviour of the fish, and particularly those which care for their young, is the most fascinating sight to be seen in the aquarium. It is also profitable as there is a ready market for most types of fish. The actual techniques for inducing fish to breed and the raising of the young are described in the next section of this book.

Egg-scatterers

Most fish which normally swim in schools, like the Barbs, Tetras, and Danios, adopt the simplest of all methods of spawning. These fish do not pair off at all, but spawn as a group. When the females are ripe with spawn, the males develop their breeding colours, which are generally much brighter than their usual coloration.

Breeding commences with prolonged chases, when the males appear to be harassing the females. When the female fish are receptive, the entire group either dashes into a bunch of fine-leaved plants, or skims close to the gravel on the tank bottom. The females shed their eggs, and simultaneously, the males pursuing them release a cloud of milt, a milky fluid containing sperms which immediately fertilize the eggs. The fertilized eggs either drift to the bottom, lodging between the particles of gravel, or may adhere to the leaves of the aquarium plants. In either case, the fish take no further interest in them, except to eat them avidly.

Spawning chases of this type often continue for many hours, and some types of fish spawn almost continually when kept in large shoals.

There is obviously a very high mortality among the eggs of fish which scatter their spawn haphazardly. Not only do the parents eat their eggs, but other fish and invertebrates such as snails also feed on them, and on the newly-hatched young. To compensate for this, such fish are extremely prolific, and in the unnatural conditions of the aquarium, huge numbers of young can be raised without difficulty.

Egg-buriers

Most of the Egg-laying Tooth Carps described in the previous chapter are egg scatterers, laying their eggs in the leaves of plants growing in small thickets. But some of the annual fish, living in puddles and swamps which dry up completely for much of the year, have to adopt a more specialized breeding technique. These fish, of the genera *Cynolebias*, *Pterolebias*, *Roloffia*, and the beautiful but quarrelsome *Nothobranchius* pair off for breeding. Males of the same species fight viciously to protect their own territory, so they must generally be kept only as mated pairs. When spawning commences, the fish dive down to the bottom of the pool or the tank, clasping one another closely, belly-to-belly. Eggs are discharged and immediately fertilized. *Pterolebias* actually dives right under the mud on the pool bottom to spawn; others spawn on the surface, burying their eggs by churning up the mud. These eggs will not hatch unless they are dried out for a prolonged period, hatching within hours of being immersed in water at a temperature of 25–27°C. These are exactly the conditions found in seasonal tropical pools and rain puddles.

Livebearers

Other Tooth Carps produce live young, as do the unrelated Halfbeaks from South East Asia. Guppies, Platies, Mollies, and Swordtails are among the easiest fish to breed in the aquarium. In these fish, the anal fin of the male is modified into a special copulatory organ called a gonopodium. Sperms are produced in the usual way, but are parcelled together into little packets called spermatophores.

Livebearers differ from most other fish in that the males, in particular, have no defined breeding season. As soon as they sense that one of the females is ripe with eggs, a male will pursue her, and carry out a complicated courtship dance. This dance varies depending on the species of fish involved, and in the wild this probably serves to prevent cross-breeding of different species.

The male is much smaller than the female, and pursues her about the tank, displaying continually, and occasionally biting at her her belly and vent. When he senses that she is suitably receptive, he extends the gonopodium sideways and copulates quickly within her, depositing a spermatophore within her vent. The female stores this spermatophore inside her body. Some of the sperms are used immediately to fertilize her eggs, which are retained and hatch within her body. When the young are born, they are up to 1cm in length, and can feed normally. The mother will eat them unless they can quickly hide among plants and stones. Remaining sperm still survive within the female's body, however, and she can give birth to several batches of young without mating again.

Several curious variants on this type of

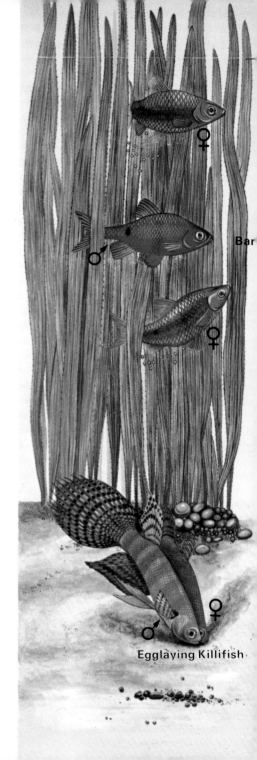

Bar

♀

♂

♀

♀

♂

Egglaying Killifish

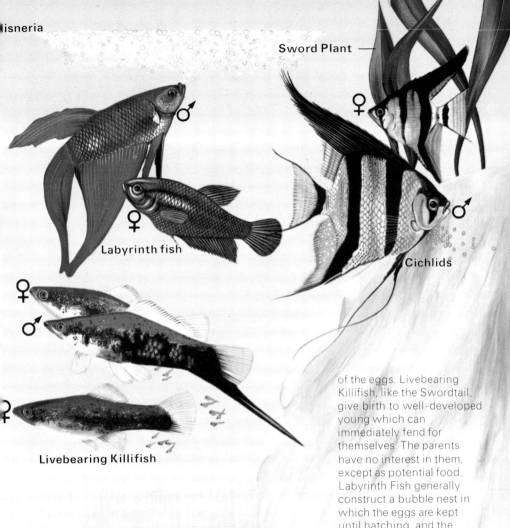

isneria

Sword Plant —

Labyrinth fish

Cichlids

Livebearing Killifish

of the eggs. Livebearing Killifish, like the Swordtail, give birth to well-developed young which can immediately fend for themselves. The parents have no interest in them, except as potential food. Labyrinth Fish generally construct a bubble nest in which the eggs are kept until hatching, and the young are guarded by the male for several days. Cichlids have even more highly developed brood care, carefully cleaning their spawning spot and driving all intruders away from their developing young. Some give them greater protection within their own mouths.

The breeding habits of freshwater fish fall into a few quite different groups.

Barbs and their relatives, the Rasboras, Danios and others, spawn as a shoal after an excited chase, depositing eggs at random in the water plants. In contrast, the small, egglaying Killifish spawn in pairs, burying their eggs in mud or peat, or sometimes suspending them from the leaves of plants, thus ensuring the survival of most breeding behaviour have been recorded. Sex changes are quite common; a fish starting out as female, and giving birth to several batches of young, may suddenly become a male which is also capable of breeding.

In the aquarium, for lack of a mate of the same species, many species of livebearer can be persuaded to interbreed, and in this way aquarists have been able to develop many beautiful hybrids, such as Swordtailed Platies, and varieties with flowing finnage.

Halfbeaks are not closely related to the Livebearing Tooth Carps, being members of the group including Flying Fish. They resemble tiny swordfish, and breed in a similar way to Guppies and Platies, being chiefly noted for the prolonged battles which take place between rival males. In parts of Indonesia they are bred for fighting, and bets are placed on the outcome.

Egg guardians

Many distantly related fish have developed the complicated habit of caring for their eggs and the young. The Cichlids are the most notable exponents of this type of breeding behaviour. Although there are many variations, the basic breeding method of Cichlids is as follows.

As fish become sexually mature, they begin to pair off. Male fish take over a territory, which they defend vigorously against all intruders, and especially against other members of their own species. Many pair for life, and having selected a mate, the two fish choose a suitable breeding spot. This is usually a stone, underwater cave, or plant leaf. The fish clean this carefully of all debris, ready for spawning. Breeding is preceded by prolonged displays of brilliant colours by the male fish, usually with all fins outspread. Some Cichlids grasp each other by the jaws and

▲ Mouthbreeding Cichlids take the whole shoal of young into their mouths for safety when danger threatens.

wrestle, or may confine themselves to threatening displays, but the courtship of Cichlids is always a potentially violent affair. The adhesive eggs are laid onto the selected site, and immediately fertilized by the male. Both fish then guard the eggs, fanning them with their fins to encourage a flow of oxygen-rich water, and removing any which become fungused. As soon as they hatch, the fry are picked up in the parents' mouths, and spat out into a pit excavated in the bottom. The tiny shoal of young fish is carefully protected by the parents until they are large enough to fend for themselves. Most Cichlids will even attack the aquarists' hand if it is placed near their young, although when disturbed some will eat the young in a panic.

Once again, there are some variations. Mouthbreeder Cichlids keep the eggs and developing young inside the mouth of one or other parent. Sometimes they pick up the fertilized eggs in order to rear them, but in other species, a more ingenious system has developed. After the female lays her eggs, she picks them up in her

▲ Like many other Cichlids, the Firemouth digs a brooding nest in the gravel and guards its young fiercely.

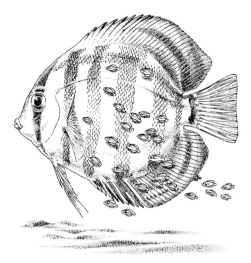

▲ The stately and temperamental Discus first spawns on a prepared site, then feeds the young on its own body slime.

mouth. The male then turns, so that his anal fin, decorated with bright spots, is displayed to his mate. She picks at the spots, apparently trying to eat them, and in doing so, ingests some of the milt which he releases, so fertilizing the eggs inside her mouth.

The stately Discus, *Symphysodon,* has a modification of the basic Cichlid method of breeding, in that the newly-hatched young feed on nutrient slime produced on their parents' bodies. Many other types of fish also guard their eggs and young in a similar manner to the Cichlids.

Bubble-nest builders

Several groups of fish, including most Labyrinth Fish and some Catfish, guard their eggs and young in a different way. A typical Labyrinth Fish, like the Siamese Fighter *Betta splendens,* or the Gouramis, starts by building a bubble nest which floats on the water surface, and is constructed by the male. When he has completed it to his satisfaction, he lures a

female to it by means of elaborate courtship displays. When the female is ready to mate, the male wraps himself about her, turning her upside down, and squeezing her so that eggs are ejected and can be fertilized. He immediately catches the eggs in his mouth, and spits them into the nest. The nest and the young are guarded from all intruders.

Egg-sprayers

One of the oddest breeding methods of all is practised by *Copeina arnoldi,* an attractive but not exceptional-looking little Characin. This fish spawns *out* of the water, on the tank cover or an overhanging leaf. Clasped together, male and female leap up out of the water, to touch the chosen spawning site. A few eggs are deposited and fertilized, then the fish drop back into the water, repeating the process several times. The male stations himself beneath the clutch of eggs, and every few seconds, flips water over them with his tail. As the eggs hatch, in about 36 hours, the fry are washed back into the water.

The marine aquarium

The dream of most aquarists is to reproduce in their home the beauty and teeming activity of the coral reef, especially since the advent of so many films and television programmes depicting underwater life. Until quite· recently, most attempts at keeping exotic marine fish were doomed to failure, largely because of outbreaks of disease, and also due to problems with the quality of the water.

This has all changed. Tropical marines are now popular and practical, although they do demand more care and understanding of their needs than their freshwater relatives. The breakthrough came about as a result of two developments. The first of these was the introduction of all-glass or all-plastic tanks, cemented together with clear silicone rubber adhesive. This allowed the traditional metal frame to be eliminated, and removed a source of serious contamination of the aquarium water. Sea water is highly corrosive to metals, and when it attacked the tank frame, iron compounds found their way into the water, which soon became toxic. The new cemented tanks have a further advantage, in that the adhesive used is resilient, so if the tank shifts slightly on its stand it is unlikely to spring a leak.

The other major advance is in the introduction of synthetic sea salts, which are mixed with tap water to provide the aquarists with sterile substitute sea water whenever it is needed. This development resulted from increasing knowledge of the actual constituents of natural sea water, which contains a vast range of chemicals. Some are present in only minute quantities, but are essential for healthy fish.

Marine fish and invertebrates are now readily available from specialist shops, and sufficient experience has now been gained for the more delicate and temperamental types to have been weeded out. Just as with freshwater fish, there are now a number of 'standard' marines, which are hardy and peaceful.

Marine fish are still very expensive compared to most freshwater types, however. The primary reason for this is that few marine fish have been bred in the aquarium, and even with those types which do breed fairly predictably, there has been little success in raising the young, chiefly due to the difficulty in providing suitable live food. Consequently, marine fish must be caught in the wild, usually on reefs in the Indo-Pacific, and flown in after becoming acclimatized to captivity. And even catching the fish can be difficult, as many tend to hide deep within the reef. Many marine tropicals are caught individually by skin divers. Fortunately, the commoner and cheaper species are also the most hardy.

From sea to aquarium

Freshwater fish are adapted to withstand some variations in their water conditions, due to seasonal rains, etc. Tropical marines live in the most stable environment imaginable, however. Temperature varies hardly at all, and as coral reefs exist well away from estuaries, the concentration of dissolved chemicals in the sea scarcely varies.

▶ *Balistoides niger*, the Clown Triggerfish, is an expensive and very aggressive specimen, in spite of its comical looks.

Consequently, marine fish, with a few exceptions, cannot withstand any appreciable variations in their aquatic habitat. We have seen how in the freshwater tank, the waste products from the fish are made harmless and are recycled by the bacteria and the plants. In the marine tank, it is usual to try to keep the conditions as near bacteria-free as possible, and marine plants are very difficult to keep in a healthy condition. So the waste products from the fish, consisting of urine and faeces, together with uneaten particles of food, can very soon disturb the chemical balance of the relatively small amount of sea water in the aquarium. A further complication is that sea water holds much less dissolved oxygen than freshwater. This in turn means that for a given volume of water, fewer fish can be kept, and that these fish will suffer from overcrowding more than will their freshwater relatives.

Taken together, this means that aeration, to increase the oxygen level, and filtration, to remove detritus, are absolutely essential for success in keeping marine fish. Waste products can be coped with in two ways.

Either by regularly removing a quantity of water, and replacing it with freshly made-up synthetic sea water, or by using a form of filtration which removes the organic wastes produced by the fish, or at any rate, makes them harmless. A third, but more difficult solution is to use chemical means to deactivate these substances, but this is difficult and expensive on the small scale of the home aquarium, although it is often adopted in large public aquaria.

There are simple test kits available which allow the aquarist to measure the chemical build-up in the tank, so that the appropriate correcting measures can be taken.

A bright and brilliant tank

The marine tank thus differs from the freshwater version in being less heavily populated, strongly aerated and filtered, and in having little or no plant life. This produces conditions very like those on the coral reef, where the water is constantly in motion, and continuously being re-

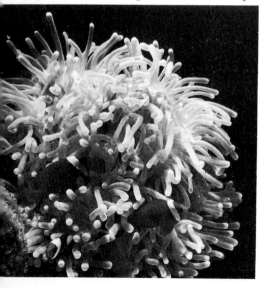

Interesting marine curiosities are the Tomato Clown (*left*), living within its sea anemone home, and the Cleaner Wrasse (*above*) which picks parasites out of larger fish.

▲ In the marine community great care must be taken that the brilliantly coloured fish are all compatible.

plenished by clean water from the open sea.

The tank can be made to look most attractive. Instead of plants, large sections of coral can be arranged at the back and sides of the tank; these also provide hiding places for the shyer species of fish. A thin covering of coral sand is usually placed on the tank bottom to minimize the available places where waste could be trapped and allow bacteria to build up.

Marine fish are used to very strong lighting in their natural habitat, so marine tanks can be brightly lit to bring out their brilliant colours. The constant motion of marines, combined with their colouring, large size and often bizarre shape, makes the marine tank an eye-catching centre-piece for the living room.

Alternative systems

Apart from the 'hygienic' marine aquarium described above, different systems have been tried. One such technique is the 'natural' system, in which chunks of living coral, invertebrates, and marine plants such as algae are placed together in a well-aerated tank, with a very thick bed of gravel. Soon everything in the tank becomes coated with an invisible layer of bacteria which neutralizes the nitrites produced by the waste products of the fish. This is a perfect miniature version of life in the open sea. But if the slightest thing goes wrong—like an animal or fish dying and not being removed immediately—the balance of the whole aquarium goes dramatically wrong, and all the contents will die very rapidly.

The other, and perhaps the easiest alternative, is to use a 'semi-natural' system with a sub-gravel filter (described in more detail on page 39 of this book). This type of filter, powered by an inexpensive pump, draws water down through a thick bed of gravel, and then discharges the filtered water, now re-oxygenated, back at the water surface. Within about a month of setting up the tank, the gravel bed will have naturally become coated with a huge number of bacteria which are capable of neutralizing all the nitrites your fish can produce.

This is in complete contrast to the bacteria-free conditions aimed at in the 'hygienic' tank, which rely on expensive and highly effective power filters and demand constant monitoring of water conditions.

Obviously the easiest, cheapest, and most satisfactory type of marine aquarium for the beginner is the semi-natural type, using the sub-gravel filter which, after a few weeks maturation, has an enormous ability to remove and neutralize any waste products. Combine this with a sensible selection of fish in a properly set up tank, and success with marines is within your grasp.

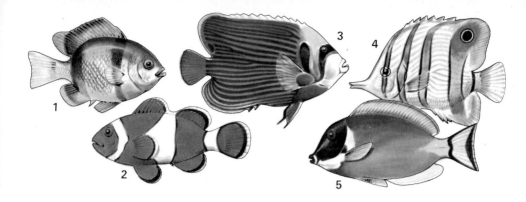

Types of marine fish

Although the range of fish living in tropical seas is almost limitless, the choice available for the home aquarist is limited by the size and habits of the fish. Many types, even those kept commonly in the aquarium, grow unnacceptably large, and can only be kept in the juvenile form. Others are fish of the open seas, visiting reefs only occasionally. In the small home aquarium, they are restless and do not thrive. In contrast, many of the small reef fishes adopt a corner of the tank as their own home, in which they rest and hide.

Most are carnivorous, requiring careful feeding, although a few appreciate a proportion of vegetable matter in their diet.

1 Damselfish or Demoiselles A group of reef fish which are ideal for the aquarist. They are relatively small in size, greedy feeders, and very active. Few of them grow to more than 15cm in length, and most will even accept dried flake food. As a group, they have one definite disadvantage, in that they are quite aggressive, driving off any intruder from the part of the tank that they have appropriated as their own. They are best kept singly, being less aggressive to other species than they are with their own kind.

2 Clownfish These share with the Damselfish the benefits of small size, but are much more brightly coloured. These are the fish so often shown living deep within the poisonous tentacles of large sea anemones, from whose sting they seem immune. In the aquarium they can also be kept together with an anemone, but this requires some special care, as like most other invertebrates, anemones may quickly die and foul the water. Clownfish are very satisfactory aquarium fish, feeding well, and even breeding in the tank on occasion.

3 Angelfish These very large (up to 60cm) and beautifully marked fish, which are quite unrelated to the freshwater Angelfish, demand more space than the average aquarist can provide. They are frequently seen in large public aquaria, but those suitable for the home aquarium are generally the juvenile forms, often entirely differently marked to the adults.

4 Butterflyfish Just as attractive as the Angelfish, Butterflyfish are much less aggressive and are of a more manageable size, up to 10cm in length. In the wild, they use their beak-like mouths to pick food out of crevices in the coral, and they also have

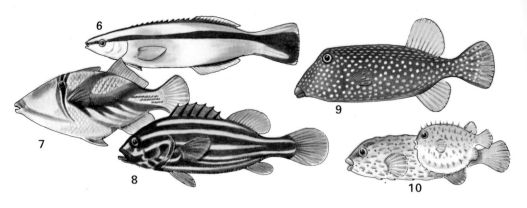

an expensive habit of browsing on living coral polyps. In general, they are rather sensitive and prone to shock, being particularly badly affected by nitrite build-up in the water, so they are best added only to a mature and well-run aquarium. Once they start feeding they are quite hardy, often relishing vegetable food.

5 Surgeonfish and Tangs In addition to their spectacular colours, these fish are notable in having a pair of razor-sharp 'scalpels' hidden at the base of their tails, which they use to good effect when being handled, and when fighting rival fish. Young fish are suitable for the community tank, but may later turn on the other occupants, usually with fatal results.

6 Wrasse A varied and hardy group of fish which are not usually too aggressive. Some have the odd habit of burying themselves in the gravel at night. All swim with a curious rowing action of the pectoral fins. The Cleaner Wrasse removes parasites from the skin of its tank-mates.

7 Triggerfish Very large, hardy, and aggressive show fish with a spike-like dorsal fin which can be locked in such a way as to wedge the fish immovably into a crevice. They have powerful beak-like jaws and feed mainly on crustaceans.

8 Groupers Although these solitary predators can grow very large, they make ideal aquarium fish, as long as they are not tempted by being kept with smaller tank-mates. They become tame enough to feed from the hand, and many species are beautifully marked.

9 Trunkfish This curious group of fish are enclosed in a rigid shell, sometimes with horns or spikes, and their immobile body is rowed along with the fins. They are peaceful, but if frightened, many will emit a poisonous slime which speedily kills their adversary, themselves, and all the other fish in the tank.

10 Puffers and Porcupine Fish These are closely related to the Trunkfish, and are able to inflate themselves enormously when threatened. Porcupine fish are covered with spines which can be erected when they become inflated.

Brackish-water fish Fish from estuaries are equally at home in freshwater, brackish water, or marine conditions. When acclimatized to sea water, they are very hardy, and are suitable subjects for the beginner. Typical examples are Scats *Scatophagus argus,* and *Monodactylus argenteus,* the Malay Angel. Several species of freshwater Pufferfish can also live in marine conditions.

The home aquarium

So far, we have considered only the technical aspects of keeping tropical fish in the home. Unfortunately, this is a hobby which means the use of a certain number of gadgets and extraneous lengths of cable, air pipes, etc., which can seriously detract from the natural beauty of the miniature underwater world within the tank. So to make your tank a thing of beauty, *and* an acceptable and attractive part of the decor, you must consider how best to display it.

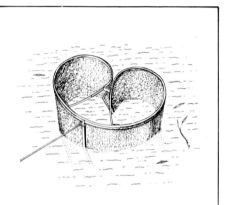

The wire basket trap is widely used by the fish collector operating in tropical areas. It is shaped so that the fish can enter, but not escape so easily. Another large-scale trapping technique is the use of very fine mesh nets which can catch an entire shoal of fish with a single sweep. After capture, saleable fish are selected and packaged in insulated polythene bags, ready for air freight.

Concealing the cables

The modern aquarium is usually supplied with an attractive lid or canopy, which is in keeping with the rest of the tank, and serves to contain the lights. If you use fluorescent lighting, which does not produce much heat, there is no reason why the air pump cannot be installed under the hood as well, avoiding at least some of the litter of pipes trailing down the side.

When this is not feasible, it is usually possible to hide pipes and electrical cables behind the tank, together with outside filters which must be hooked onto the tank side. It is worthwhile strapping all the trailing pipes and wires together with plastic tape to keep them tidy, and prevent aerators, heaters, and so on from being dislodged when cleaning the tank.

Modern tanks, and particularly the types made of glass cemented together at the edges, are starkly simple in appearance, and if tidily installed can do much to enhance the appearance of a room. Special stands are available to carry one or more tanks at a suitable height from the floor, but never forget the weight of such a set-up, especially if the floor of your room is weak or uneven. An average sized aquarium can weigh around 150kg; put two or more on a stand, complete with air pumps and other equipment, and you may have a major disaster. Check the floors first!

Custom-built tanks

As the all-glass tanks are so easily made, it is worth considering ordering one specially designed to fit a convenient alcove, such as an unused cupboard, or the space alongside

a chimney breast. Simple covers can be made to conceal the cables and lighting fittings, leaving only the tank itself exposed.

You can be a little more adventurous, and use a very large tank as a room divider, as water depths of up to 70cm are quite feasible, provided you remember that the deeper the water, the more powerful must be the pump used for aeration and filtration, and the stronger the lights used to allow the plants to grow.

The life within the tank must also be taken into account when designing your display. In a large tank, intended to be viewed from a distance, large fish are more appropriate than the small types kept by the average aquarist. In a large tank used as a room divider, you should consider large and active fish, allowing them plenty of swimming space between groups of well-rooted plants.

For a smaller tank, stood on a sideboard or strong shelf, you may prefer some of the smaller, brightly coloured fish in a heavily planted environment which makes the shyer species feel more secure.

▲ When a large tank is used as a room divider, it is usually possible to conceal unsightly cables and air lines.

Contrasting colours

Don't feel restricted to decorating your tank only with gravel, plants and rock. Water-worn branches and roots, for example, make an attractive contrast to the bright green of the aquarium plants. Sheets of slate and other types of rock can also add to the beauty of the display, if necessary being cemented together with aquarium silicone sealant to prevent them from being dislodged by the fish.

Whatever you use as decoration, make very sure that it is thoroughly cleaned. Before placing any rock in a freshwater tank, pour a little vinegar on the rock. If after a few minutes it begins to effervesce, do not use it; the rock is calcereous and will dissolve slightly making the water very hard. If there is no effervescence, wash the vinegar off the rock; it can be safely put in the tank.

Choice of equipment

The aquarist's hobby is one which is set about, more than most others, with expensive gadgetry. Some of these gadgets are genuine technical breakthroughs, others can be simply adapted from readily available materials, and others again, like plastic divers and 'wrecks' are a matter of personal taste—or lack of it. Before you rush to buy the latest 'innovation', stop and ask yourself whether it has any real or promised benefit to you or to your fish. If not, you would do better to invest money in a more spacious tank, some unusual plants, or some coveted fish.

Buying the tank

Choice of the right tank is the most important decision you can make when setting out on this new hobby. The golden rule is; *buy the largest you can afford*. Of course, you must also check that you have a suitable position for a large tank, and that your floors will take the weight.

You can choose from the traditional steel-framed tank with puttied glass, or the more modern variants with aluminium, stainless steel, or nylon-coated frames. These latter have the benefit of being corrosion-resistant, and are more attractive than the older type.

Another alternative is a plastic tank; either moulded from one piece of plastic, or cemented together, often with coloured sides and an attractively curved front. These are simple to maintain, and do not leak, but are easily scratched, so that vision through the front is soon impaired.

Probably the best type is the modern all-glass tank, cemented together with in-

▼ The amount of space each fish needs is roughly determined by its length. Use this chart as a simple guide to avoid overcrowding in your tank (volume of the tank in litres equals height x breadth x length in centimetres, divided by 1000).

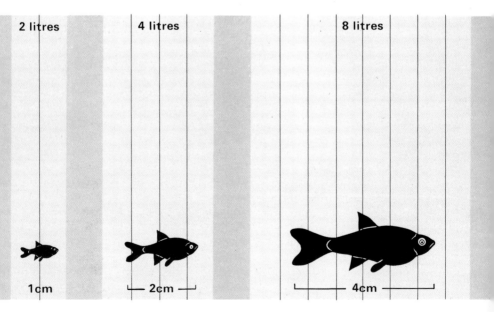

2 litres   4 litres   8 litres

1cm   2cm   4cm

credibly strong silicone rubber, and having no unsightly frame at all, although sometimes a purely decorative frame is added. These tanks are very cheap, and can be obtained or made to special order in almost any size required. And best of all, they need no maintenance. There is no putty to dry out, leaks are almost unheard of, and there will be no corrosion problems. If you are going to keep marine fish, these tanks are a must.

All-glass tanks are made by cementing plate glass together at the edge with adhesive resembling that used for sealing around the edges of baths. It *can* be done by the amateur, but the risks of failure outweigh the possible savings in cost.

You will need to buy or make a very strong stand. These are usually made from angle iron, with provision for a second tank on a lower shelf, or from plate glass, which is more decorative.

If you decide to use one of the all-glass tanks, you must support its base with strips of expanded polystyrene, which can be cut from a ceiling tile. This absorbs any slight irregularities in the base, and prevents the tank from cracking.

The cover
Your tank will also require a close-fitting cover, which has several functions. It prevents expensive fish from jumping out, and stops dust from settling on the water surface. It also reduces evaporation from the water,

which is especially important in marine aquaria, as this would increase the salinity. If you use aeration, or a filter powered by an air pump, a certain amount of spray will be produced above the water surface, and the cover will prevent this from splashing over the floor.

The cover is simply a sheet of glass or plastic cut

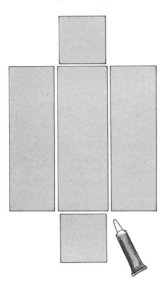

▲ Five pieces of plate glass, cemented with silicone rubber, make up the modern tank.

▲ The same adhesive makes a sealing fillet in a leaky tank.

to fit closely over the tank top. Allowance must be made to let cables and air lines pass under the edge of the cover, and many people prefer a two-part cover with a narrow strip of glass at the front of the tank, which can be lifted to feed the fish without disturbing the main cover.

Lighting
Lighting is a critical part of your aquarium. Contrary to the views of many beginners, sunlight is not at all desirable; in fact, if any sunlight falls on the tank, a heavy overgrowth of algae will probably result. Lights are fitted into a metal or plastic canopy which rests on the tank. The position of the lights within the canopy can be varied, but it is best to situate them at the front of the tank, so they shine *back* towards the fish, bringing out their colours to the full. If the lights are behind the fish, they are silhouetted against it, and lose most of

▲ Light fittings placed well forward shine light back at the fish, and enhance their colours.

their colouration. There is one other alternative, which is to use a spotlight, situated at a distance from the tank.

In the freshwater aquarium lights serve the essential function of stimulating

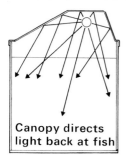

Canopy directs light back at fish

the plant growth. With too little light they become spindly and weak; with too much light, the tank speedily becomes filled with unsightly green algae. In the marine tank there is less need for light, as plants are not usually grown. Paradoxically however, marine fish are used to much brighter lighting than are freshwater fish, even though with a high level of light, some algal growth will occur.

Ordinary incandescent bulbs can be used for lighting, but they suffer from some disadvantages. The heat they generate can raise the temperature of the surface water to an unacceptable level, and as these bulbs are not designed to operate horizontally in the restricted area beneath the canopy, their life will be short.

Fluorescent tubes are much more satisfactory, being very compact, and not producing much heat. Unfortunately, the usual white types do not contain sufficient of the red spectrum of light which is essential for plant growth. Warm white tubes are better, but best of all are the new tubes specially developed for horticultural use, such as 'Gro-Lux'. These produce a rather strange-looking mauvish light, which stimulates plant growth enormously, and at the same time makes the colours of the fish stand out as though they were luminous. In the marine tank, they may encourage an overgrowth of algae, so they can be combined with ordinary white fluorescent tubes, giving a more natural appearance.

Bottom filter

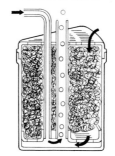

You will have to determine the power of the lights needed for your own tank by trial and error. A general rule is to allow at least two watts from an incandescent lamp or one watt from a fluorescent for each square decimetre of water surface

Outside filter

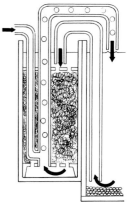

(approximately $15\frac{1}{2}$ sq ins). This is only a rough guide, as with increasing water depth, much stronger lights will be required. Watch the plants; they will tell you in their own way when the light level is correct.

Leave the lighting on for about 12 hours each day, and try to switch room lights on first if the room is dark, to avoid startling the fish too much.

Whichever form of lighting you decide to use, make very sure that the metal

Biological filter

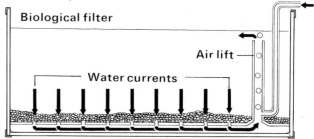

Water currents

Air lift

canopy and all equipment beneath it is properly earthed. There will be a good deal of condensation about, which can cause leakage of electricity.

Filtration

Although the 'balanced' and self-supporting aquarium is theoretically possible, in practice, effective filtration is indispensible. Most filters depend on the lifting power of air bubbles. The air is pumped through a plastic tube to the bottom of the tank, where it is released into another tube, either as large bubbles, or a fine spray of tiny bubbles. As it rises up the tube, air carries water with it, causing a continuous current up the tube. This current can be utilized for a number of useful tasks.

In the simple bottom filter, a plastic box is packed with synthetic fibre (not glass wool; this is dangerous to the fish). A layer of activated charcoal can also be included. The filter box is stood in an inconspicuous corner of the tank, where as the air lift operates, water is drawn in and solid wastes are trapped. The filter must be changed periodically.

A more efficient variant is the outside filter, which is hung over the side of the tank and is easier to clean. It has the further advantage of not being so unsightly as the internal type.

The greatest advance in filtration has been the perfection of the biological filter, also known as a sub-gravel filter. This is extremely simple, consisting of a perforated plate or system of perforated tubes, with an airlift attached to one corner. The plate or tubes are placed on the tank bottom, and covered with at least 5cm of gravel of the grade sold for aquarium use. As the airlift operates, a water current passes down into the gravel, taking solid particles down to the plant roots where they can be used. But dissolved impurities are also removed, because after a few weeks a rich population of bacteria develops on the gravel particles, which can break down almost all the waste products produced by the fish. However, the air pump must be run continuously as otherwise these useful bacteria will die and be replaced by others which cause the water to become foul.

One other type of filter is the power filter, which, by means of an electric pump, forces water through a tightly-packed filter medium. These pumps can speedily remove all suspended material from the water, but are extremely expensive and

Vibrator pump

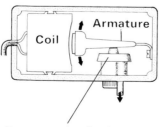

Pump mechanism

only necessary for the specialist with many tanks to care for.

All these types of filters aerate the water at the same time as cleaning it, and provide useful circulation of the water.

Air pumps

The simplest and cheapest type of air pump is known aptly as a 'vibrator'. It operates by means of an electromagnet, which causes a metal armature to vibrate up and down at very high speed. This in turn works a rubber bellows or diaphragm which delivers a flow of air to the aquarium. It has tiny one-way valves which can easily become clogged, reducing the air output, so it is important to change the air filter on the pump regularly to prevent dust build-up. Vibrators can be obtained in various sizes, some with regulators to vary the air output. They have one serious disadvantage, in that many produce a particularly offensive hum, which cannot always be shut out by hiding the pump away. If your pump is noisy, try wrapping it in porous insulating material like fibreglass loft insulation.

Motor-driven piston pumps are much quieter, and have a larger air output. They are also much more expensive, but are useful for the larger and deeper tanks now so popular, where greater pressures are necessary to cope with the increased depths of water.

One further type is the rotary pump which provides very high volumes of air, but at low pressures. For the aquarist setting up his first tank, the vibrator pump is probably the best investment, as there are few parts to go wrong, and repairs are likely to be limited to replacement of an inexpensive plastic or rubber diaphragm.

Heaters

Whatever else you may save money on, don't economize on heating your aquarium. Buy the best heater and thermostat you can afford—it is the only insurance against expensive losses in event of a failure.

The earliest types of heater have scarcely been bettered today. They consist of a spiral heating element, wound round a ceramic holder, which is hermetically sealed in a glass tube and can be safely submerged in the tank. They can be bought in various wattages, and a general rule of thumb is to use about 100 watts per 90 litres in a normally heated room. Tanks in cold or draughty situa-tions will need a higher wattage for the same volume of water.

The heater or heaters are switched on and off by a pre-set thermostat. This can be submerged, like the heater, or in small tanks can be combined with the heater in a single unit. Another type, which is easier to adjust, is stuck to the outside of the glass. All thermostats operate by the movement of a temperature-sensitive metal strip which opens and closes the contacts.

The thermometer

To monitor the temperature of the aquarium you must have a thermometer. Traditional types are floated in the water, or attached to the glass with a sucker. Other dial types can be stuck on the glass, inside or out. The easiest to use are the new plastic strip thermometers containing liquid crystals, which change colour to indicate the temperature exactly, at a glance. These are durable and unbreakable, and can be stuck inconspicuously to the front glass.

▶ The all-glass tank (1) is the easiest of all to maintain. It should not leak if handled carefully and placed on thin foam to minimize surface irregularities. You will need a net (2) to remove or transfer sick fish. The biological or under-gravel filters (3) are indispensible aids in tank maintenance. Inside or outside filters (4, 5) remove all the larger particles of dirt and mulm, used together with filter medium (6) and charcoal (7). Use a thermometer (8) to keep an accurate check on water temperature. Specially cleaned and water-worn branches (9) are an attractive aid in decorating the tank, especially when used together with modern plastic plants (10). Many different types of gravel or planting medium can be used (11) and the correct choice is especially important for the marine tank. The fluorescent tube (12) allows excellent plant growth and shows the fish off well. For the smaller tank a combined heater/thermostat (13) will be quite adequate. An effective pump (14) is necessary to run filters and to operate an aquarium 'vacuum cleaner' (15) which cleans up material too large for the filters. For the more advanced aquarist, water test kits (16) are useful, while glass cleaners (17), planting sticks (18) and microworm feeders (19) are basic aids which should always be available.

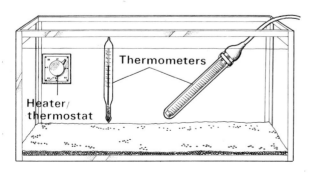

Thermometers

Heater/thermostat

Setting up the freshwater tank

When you set up your aquarium, you must have *everything* you need to hand. Once you have begun to equip your tank, you can't change your mind and decide to fit a biological filter—this would mean starting all over again. Your best course is to browse around a specialist shop dealing in tropical fish and equipment; not just an ordinary pet shop. Look at the equipment the dealer uses; ask his advice about filters, heaters, gravel quality, and types of fish and plants which will thrive in the local water. Then buy wisely, and don't be too ambitious at the start.

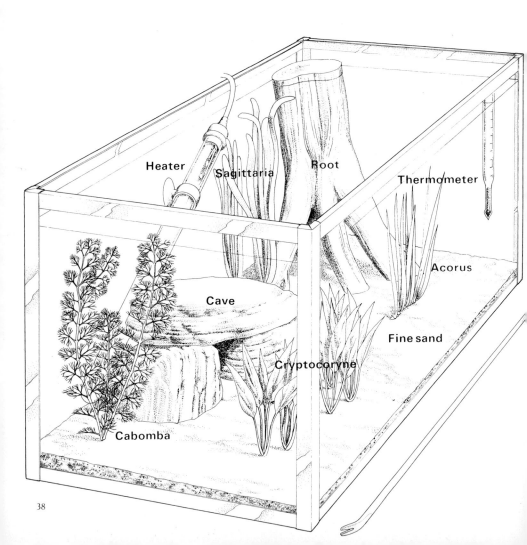

Heater Sagittaria Root Thermometer Acorus Cave Fine sand Cryptocoryne Cabomba

Assuming you have already bought your aquarium, and placed it in the spot where it is to stand (remember — you must *never* try to move a tank with water in it), the next step is to place the gravel in position. If you are going to use a biological filter, you must instal this first, of course. The best type of gravel for use in freshwater aquaria is probably freshly washed river sand, consisting of particles about 1.5–4mm in diameter ($\frac{1}{16}$ to $\frac{3}{8}$ inch).

You will need sufficient gravel to cover the filter with at least 4cm depth over the shallowest part. Before placing the gravel in the tank, it must be washed, although in theory it should be clean. This is simply done by placing the gravel, a few kilos at a time, in a plastic bucket, and either letting cold water from the tap run into it, or using a hose. A surprising amount of loose dirt will be washed away, and the process is speeded up if the gravel is stirred about with the hands.

Installing the filter
Place the biological filter into the tank, in accordance with the manufacturers' instructions. It is generally reckoned that for optimum efficiency a filter, or combination of small filters, should be used which will effectively fill the bottom of the tank, so no 'dead' areas will occur where filtration is not drawing water through the gravel.

Fit the air lines to the filter, as to do this later might disturb your entire set-up by dislodging the filter plate or pipes. Now the gravel can be added, banking it slightly towards the back of the tank. Don't bother to make too much of a slope; the fish will soon make the tank bottom quite flat and level by digging in the gravel for food.

Rocks and terraces
Now you must consider if you want to add fancy rockwork and terraces. These have several functions. Grottoes and caves look very attractive. They also provide hiding places for the shyer fish, and for nocturnal species. Oddly enough, the more hiding places there are, the less inclined the fish are to use them, presumably because they feel more secure. The most important function of rockwork is to hold back the gravel into terraces of different levels, adding an appearance of depth to the tank.

Most aquarists sell rock of a suitable quality for the aquarium. This means that the stone will not dissolve in the aquarium water to any appreciable extent, and the tank environment will therefore not be drastically altered by it. Don't use local stone unless you know that it is inert. Granite and basalt, for instance, are quite safe, but chalk and limestone have a dramatic effect on the aquarium water, dissolving rapidly to produce very

high pH values, and making water very alkaline. Water-worn wood is generally safe to use, and very attractive. Accept the advice of your local dealer as to suitable materials for the water in your area.

Large stones tend to be dislodged in the tank, and may fall against the glass. Insure against this by securing them in place with a dab of aquarium silicone sealant, and also build up terraces and walls in the same way. You can now fill the small pockets of stonework with gravel, in the same way as building a garden rockery.

Filling with water
The tank can now be partly filled. Stand a plate on the gravel, or alternatively, cover it with a large sheet of paper. Begin to pour water gently onto the plate or the paper. You will probably need a hose for this, as it takes innumerable buckets of water to fill a large tank. Use

Beginning to fill the tank

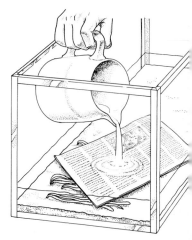

cold water; the hot water from the tap probably contains copper toxic to fish. The plate or sheet of paper will prevent the current of water from disturbing the gravel you have arranged.

The heating system

Your tank will have to stand undisturbed for a couple of days to let dissolved chlorine escape from the water. Meanwhile, you must set up the heating system. If you use a combined thermostat/heater, it need only be connected in the manner recommended by the manufacturer. If you decide to use separate thermostat and heaters, you must be prepared to do some electrical work. The thermostat will be either suspended inconspicuously at the back of the tank, or stuck externally, on the glass. To it are wired the heater cables, using small insulated plastic terminal blocks. Suspend the heaters in the tank, hooking their

cables over the side, to support them in position. Bend the cables so that the heaters are as near as possible to the tank bottom, lying horizontally, but *not quite touching* the gravel.

Having made sure that the heater and thermostat are installed *exactly* as recommended, switch on and wait for the water to heat up. The thermostat should be preset, but check with your thermometer, and adjust it if necessary, remembering to switch off at the mains before you do so, and allowing at least 12 hours for the temperature to stabilize. The cables and air pipe can be clipped together, using a piece of insulating tape to keep them tidy.

The air pump

Connect up the air pump to the pipe supplying the filter, and switch on. Almost certainly, there will be a rush of air which foams at the surface. Most pumps have a

valve with which their output can be regulated, and the flow should be cut back until a regular stream of bubbles is produced, which does not disturb the water too much. If your pump has no adjuster, fit a separate clamp or air valve into the plastic pipe. The pump can be hidden behind the tank, but not below it. Otherwise, when you switch off, the rapidly cooling air inside the pump mechanism will suck water up the pipe, and syphon most of the tank contents over the floor. Keep the pump above the tank, if possible; otherwise disconnect the pipe when switching off.

If your pump has a high enough capacity, you can use this to run additional filters. Inside types can be concealed behind the rockwork; others are suspended behind the tank.

Having got so far, the back of the tank will look rather stark. You can purchase plastic underwater scenes, and sculptured rockwork, which attach to the back of the tank, and serve to hide the cables, as well as giving an illusion of greater depth.

Lighting

The lights can now be fitted. Don't forget that to bring out the best colours in your fish, lights must be at the *front* of the tank; shining back at the fish. If there is a choice of bulb holders in the tank canopy, use the one nearest the front. Make absolutely certain that all the lighting

▼ Rock terraces allow gravel banks to remain stable even when the fish dig.

▼ Choice plants can be protected behind a glass screen to protect them from herbivorous fish.

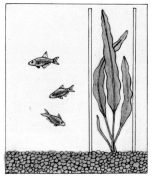

equipment is properly installed, and remember that *it must be properly earthed*. It is a very good idea to earth all the metal parts of your set-up, including the tank frame, if you are using a metal-framed aquarium.

Bearing in mind that at some time you are bound to splash water about, and that the bubbles produced by the filter will produce a fine spray, make quite sure that there are no gaps in the light and heating fittings where water could penetrate. Condensation can easily run down a cable and into an unprotected electrical fitting. If there is any possibility of this happening, seal the fittings with silicone rubber sealant, which should make them completely safe.

Plant life
The final step is to add the plants; the features which bring the whole tank to life.

Don't fall into the trap of calling them 'water weed' or you will mortally offend the experienced aquarist. Plants grown especially for tropical aquariums are carefully cultivated from imported wild forms, and are every bit as exotic and spectacular as are indoor foliage plants.

Aquarium plants can be loosely divided into two groups; those which produce large amounts of oxygen during the daylight hours, and a purely decorative group which produce little oxygen. Oxygenating plants were formerly recommended for setting up 'balanced' tanks, where theoretically, no aeration or filtration would be necessary. This type of tank is not generally easy to maintain, but the same group of plants still has application in the newly set-up tank. The oxygenating plants grow very rapidly, and are conse-

quently very cheap. They can speedily fill unsightly gaps in your new tank, while more desirable decorative plants, which grow quite slowly, are establishing themselves. This type of plant not only grows fast, but soon becomes stringy and untidy, unless kept in absolutely the best conditions. They are probably best kept as temporary planting for the tank.

Fast-growing plants
Typical fast-growing plants are *Cabomba*, *Myriophyllum*, *Ambulia*, *Elodea*, *Hygrophila*, and *Ludwigia*; all plants with smallish leaves, which are best planted in

▼ In a really well-planted tank, plants can be as attractive as the fish, although they may take months to become well established.

bunches. These plants root themselves very rapidly, and nipped-off sections can be simply pushed into the gravel, where they will take root within a few days. Fish tend to dislodge these 'bunch' plants, and they are often supplied with plant anchors, pieces of lead strip which should have no harmful effects, wrapped around the bunch to hold it in place. Even lead dissolves to some extent, however, and this is best removed, and the plants secured with a small stone until they are well rooted.

Vallisneria and *Sagittaria* are grass-like plants, which grow to form dense thickets. They spread quickly once established, by means of runners which push their way beneath the gravel.

Although not particularly attractive on their own, these plants make a good screen for the back and sides of the tank, and, as there are several species available, can be selected to form groups of varying height.

Decorative plants

There is a very large choice of specimen plants to make a decorative centrepiece for the tank. Some plants grow very large and to be seen at their best demand a spacious tank with deep water. The larger Amazon Swords *Echinodorus* species, *Aponogeton*, and the Spatterdock *Nymphaea*, spread out to fill smaller tanks. They are greedy feeders, and consequently help to dispose of nitrogenous wastes produced by the fish, just as do

the fast-growing oxygenating plants.

There is a very large range of smaller and more manageable decorative plants which come in a wide variety of shapes and colours, and sizes, and with these most attractive tank layouts can be created.

Among the dark-leaved plants which provide contrast with the brighter greens of oxygenating plants, the most valuable are the *Cryptocorynes*, which grow quite slowly, but eventually produce dense thickets in which the fish will find shelter. Some of the *Cryptocorynes* have attractively marbled foliage, and others have a brilliant wine-red colouration on the underside of their leaves.

As with *Sagittaria* and

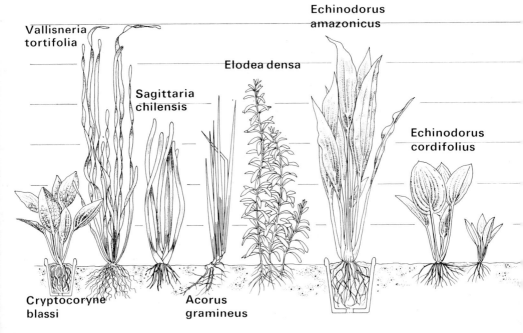

Vallisneria tortifolia

Sagittaria chilensis

Elodea densa

Echinodorus amazonicus

Echinodorus cordifolius

Cryptocoryne blassi

Acorus gramineus

Echinodorus, there are dwarf species of *Cryptocoryne*, and these are especially useful for planting in the foreground of the tank, where they will not obscure either fish or the other plants.

Planting is simplicity itself; the plants are pushed into the gravel, leaving the crown, or section from which the leaves grow, exposed on the surface, while all the roots are covered. Large plants will need several stones to hold down their roots and prevent the plant from floating out of the gravel. Some especially choice plants which need rich compost can be grown in small flowerpots, filled with peat. The peat must be covered with gravel to prevent it spreading about the tank. The pot itself can be concealed behind stonework or buried in deep pockets of gravel.

Arranging the plants

Remember, to give an illusion of a natural pool or stream, you must create an appearance of depth in your arrangement. This means that small plants must be kept at the front of the tank, and larger plants at the back and sides. Clumps of larger plants *can* be planted near the front, as long as you leave avenues or gaps between them so that plants and rockwork towards the back of the tank can be seen.

Try to plant in groups except in the cases of very large plants. Slow-growing plants like *Cryptocoryne* do not thrive when grown too close to more vigorous plants like *Sagittaria* and *Vallisneria*. Similarly, small fine-leaved plants are easily choked by sediment and should be grown near the filter outlet, where water currents keep them clean.

When making your selection of plants, bear in mind that some fish nip the leaves, or may even graze them down to stumps. Other fish, like Cichlids, dig in the gravel and uproot plants. You can get round this problem by growing only coarse-leaved plants like the larger species of *Echinodorus*; by placing a sheet of glass to separate the plants from the fish; dispensing with plants altogether, and substituting arrangements of rocks and weathered wood; or finally by using plastic plants.

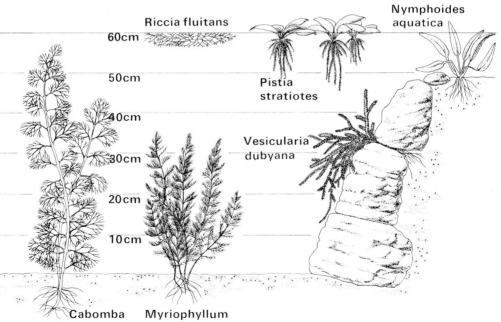

Nymphoides
aquatica

Riccia fluitans

60cm

50cm

Pistia
stratiotes

40cm

Vesicularia
dubyana

30cm

20cm

10cm

Cabomba   Myriophyllum

Intro-ducing the fish

Now your aquarium is set up and ready for the fish. Hopefully you will have let it stand for at least a couple of days to allow chlorine in the tap water to escape into the air, and also checked that the temperature has stabilized to the proper figure, which is generally about 22–26°C (72–79°F). Some fish, and the new importations from Africa especially, prefer temperatures at the top end of this band, or even higher. Having carefully checked that your tank is properly set up, you are ready to go out and buy the fish.

Before you rush off to the nearest stockist of tropical fish, sit down quietly, and decide carefully just which fish you are going to need. Do you want a few large species, for example, like Angelfish or Gouramis? Or are you going to purchase small shoals of the pretty Tetras? You may not be able to mix them, as Angelfish will make short work of small tankmates like Neon or Cardinal Tetras.

Make a list of possible purchases, and don't buy on

▼ Netting fish demands patience and care if the fish are not to be panicked and possibly injured.

impulse—it could be an expensive mistake.

Transporting fish
Now you must consider how you will transport your purchases. For small fish, a wide-mouthed vacuum flask is a suitable temporary home, but most stockists now supply fish in polythene bags, partially inflated and secured with a plastic clip or a rubber band. These are compact and watertight, but do cool off very rapidly—and a sudden chill is a certain way to bring on disease in apparently healthy fish.

The most efficient way to carry your fish is simply to place their bag in an insulated container made of expanded polystyrene which can be purchased quite cheaply in frozen food shops. It is advisable to pack them with screwed up newspaper, fitting snugly around the bags of fish to stop cooling air from circulating. If you don't have access to such a container, improvize one from scrap polystyrene foam stuck together with ceiling tile adhesive. Failing this, wrap the bag up

in a scarf or an old coat to keep it warm.

These precautions may sound pedantic, but many diseases lie dormant, suppressed by the natural immunity of the fish. When the fish are weakened by chills or by shock, the disease flares up as if by magic. So carry your fish carefully, and get them home quickly.

Health
The fish you choose *should* be healthy, if they are bought from a reputable dealer.

▼ Fish are generally packed in sealed polythene bags for transport. Make sure they are kept warm enough.

▲ Float the bag unopened in the tank for half an hour to equalize the temperatures.

▲ Allow small amounts of tank water to enter before gently tipping in the fish.

However, choose the specimen *you* want and insist on the dealer catching that one, even if this takes a lot of manoeuvering with the net. In general, the healthiest fish are those with the brightest colours, and with the fins fully spread. Avoid any fish which loiters in the tank corner with folded fins, or which hangs about near the surface. Especially avoid fish which are thin, have sunken sides, or with a blackish colouration on their bodies —they are probably dying. Examine the other fish in the tank, and look carefully for the pin-head sized white speckles of White Spot Disease, which is regrettably endemic in some dealers' tanks. Your fish are bound to catch White Spot at some time, but take all possible precautions to avoid it for as long as possible.

Introducing the fish
The first thing to do once you have bought your fish is to introduce them carefully into the tank. Float their plastic bag in the tank for at least an hour, to allow the temperature to equalize with that of the tank. It is most unlikely that the water chemistry of the dealer's tank is the same as that in your newly set-up tank, so it is necessary to change the water in the bag very slowly, adding small amounts of water from the tank, over a period of at least half-an-hour, or preferably much longer. In this way, differences in pH and dissolved solids will be slowly evened out without damaging the delicate gills and kidneys of the fish.

However carefully you add the fish to your tank, they will look very unhappy for a while. Turn the lights out, and leave them overnight to get used to their new home. A feed with live daphnia will soon make even the shyest fish feel at home.

What happens if you already have an established tank? It is advisable to quarantine new fish, before adding them to an existing populated tank, and the cheapest way to do this is to purchase a simple one-piece plastic tank, which will need no gravel or plants. This can be used solely for quarantine and as a 'hospital' tank, being equipped with only a heater and thermostat. If your new fish harbour White Spot or any other common disease, it will show up within three days. If they are clear after this time, add them to the tank in the same way as before.

When you add new fish to an established community, there will probably be a certain amount of harassment of the new arrivals by the original fish. It is a good idea to divert their attention by giving them a good feed when the new fish are introduced.

If you do have problems of new fish failing to thrive it might be worth testing the nitrite levels in your tank. The existing fish may have become acclimatized to them; the shock may be too much for new fish, however.

Foods and feeding

Tropical fish will eat a surprising variety of foods. Don't restrict them to the convenient dried foods, or digestive troubles may result. Nearly all fish are carnivorous, and most enjoy the young fry of livebearers (including the parents). Other fish, like Mollies, need some vegetable material in their diet, and will nibble on pieces of lettuce. But whatever food you use, don't ever give more than the fish will eat completely within five minutes, or you risk fouling the water. The only exceptions to this golden rule are live worms given from a feeder, which are 'rationed out' and take a long while to be eaten.

Dried foods are the standby for the home aquarium. Not old-fashioned ants' eggs or dried daphnia, but the modern, carefully formulated foods, which are available in different sized flakes or granules to suit the largest mouths or tiny fish fry. Special types can be obtained for fish needing a vegetable supplement to their diet.

It is always better to buy a more expensive brand of dried food, which contains all the ingredients needed to keep your fish in perfect health. Floating foods are useful, as they minimize the risk of missing food particles which would decay.

Daphnia are tiny crustaceans which are available live from most dealers. They are very nutritious and hardly any fish will refuse them. Use as part of a mixed diet or the fish may refuse to eat other foods, and in the winter, when Daphnia are difficult to obtain, this can cause problems.

Tubifex are small red worms which are collected from shallow water contaminated by sewage. They are a good food for fish, but obviously require careful cleaning to avoid introducing disease. The compact ball of Tubifex worms should be left in a jar under a slowly running tap for a day before use, which should make them safe to use. Uneaten worms live in the gravel and may look most unsightly.

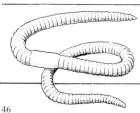

Earthworms make a very good food if chopped finely. They are especially relished by predatory fish like Cichlids, although most fish will eat them if they are chopped finely enough. After chopping the worms, rinse them thoroughly in a net to remove slime and earth.

Brine shrimp are also crustaceans, which live naturally in the salt lakes of the USA. Their eggs are sold by dealers, and can be hatched in salt water. Newly hatched brine shrimp are a valuable food for young fish, and the adults are relished by all large fish, but are difficult to produce. It is possible to cultivate brine shrimp on the window-sill in jam-jars, from a kit purchased from a dealer, but if you have a freezer, it is much easier to buy blocks of frozen adult shrimps, which can be crushed and used as needed. Frozen brine shrimp are an essential diet for most marine fish. Living adult shrimp will survive in the marine tank until needed.

White worms and Grindal worms are small terrestrial worms which are useful because they can be cultured easily, and so are available when needed. 2cm-long White worms are grown in boxes of damp earth, feeding on pieces of bread placed on the surface. They are scraped off when needed and used from a worm feeder. Grindal worms, which are smaller, are fed on moist porridge. Renew cultures after 6-8 weeks.

Microworms are so small as to be almost invisible, and are an indispensible food for raising fry. They are cultured in glass jars, being fed on oatmeal and milk. As the worms multiply, they creep up the side of the jar, and can easily be scraped off with the finger and rinsed into the rearing tank.

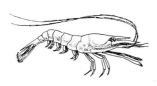

Shrimps and fish eggs make useful additions to the diet of your fish. Use only fresh-cooked shrimps, not the potted type, and suspend one in the tank on a thread so the fish can pick at it. Eggs are often found in fish being cleaned for the table, and on the underside of shrimps, and are relished by the fish in small quantities.

Other livefoods can be obtained to vary the diet of your fish. Mosquito larvae and small jointed bloodworms from rainwater tubs or puddles make excellent food and form a large part of the diet of wild fish. Freshly swatted flies are relished by larger fish, and smaller species will eat aphids or greenfly brushed from garden plants—but beware toxic insecticides.

Breeding and rearing

Breeding fish successfully demands a good deal of preparation and understanding of their needs. A few fish breed even in the community tank. Some, like Guppies and Swordtails, will breed almost continually, although their fry are usually eaten. In many other cases, breeding can lead to trouble in the tank, as fish frequently get very aggressive and begin to attack their tankmates. As soon as your fish begin courting behaviour, separate them into another, specially prepared tank, and make sure you have another tank available for rearing the young.

Development

Angelfish start out as quite ordinary looking young which rapidly develop the exaggerated finnage of the adults.

• actual size

Newly hatched larva 4mm

9 days 7mm

20 days 12mm

36 days 18mm

General principles

Fish eggs and very young fry are particularly susceptible to diseases caused by bacteria and fungi, so it is important to eliminate these. Hydrogen peroxide solution is a good sterilizing agent for tanks and equipment. It quickly breaks down into harmless residues and is easily rinsed off after use with running water.

Your adult fish will be acclimatized to the water in their usual tank, so transfer as much of this water as possible to their breeding quarters. If the fish have special requirements in water chemistry, such as very hard or very soft water, now is the time to gradually adjust the water conditions. The fish are much more likely to breed successfully, if conditions are as close as possible to those of their natural habitat.

Marine fish are a difficult proposition for the amateur aquarist to breed. Damselfish and Clownfish frequently pair-off and spawn in the manner of the freshwater Cichlids, producing huge numbers of eggs. Although these hatch satisfactorily, it is very difficult to feed them, and the fry seldom survive.

Feeding young fish

To ensure survival of the maximum number of fry, you must feed the right size and quality of food. Some young fish can immediately eat dried foods, of a special grade produced in dust-like form. The classic food for the youngest fish is Infusoria; a culture of microscopic organisms prepared by soaking chopped hay in water for 2-3 days. The organisms colour the water as a pinkish haze, and can be transferred to the breeding tank in an eye dropper or a small spoon, as soon as the fish hatch. Use only tiny amounts, for they die off very quickly. As the young fish grow, transfer them to a diet of newly hatched brine shrimp and dried foods or the special grades for fry.

Livebearers

Easiest of all fish to breed, livebearers offer the aquarist the opportunity to hybridize and produce his own strain of Guppies, Platies, etc. From a single mating, a female livebearer will produce four or five broods, so the pair can be separated after mating. For breeding, a small tank about 30cm x 20cm x 20cm is sufficient, and the moulded one-piece plastic type is ideal. The young, about 5mm long, are expelled a few at a time, and they promptly seek cover from their mother. A thick screen of floating plants will protect some of the fry from their cannibalistic mother, but if you want to save most of the young, a spawning trap is essential. This can be made from two sheets of glass or plastic, cut to fit the tank and supported in a wedge position as shown in the diagram. The pregnant female should be placed in the trap when the young can be seen as a large dark patch on her abdomen, and fed well with live daphnia or brine shrimp. As she gives birth the young escape through the bottom of the trap. A length of garden plastic netting can also be used as a trap, although the mesh size (less than 8mm) must be carefully selected to stop the mother escaping through the holes. After birth is complete, remove the mother and feed her well to build her up for the next brood. The young can be reared in the breeding tank, and can be fed brine shrimp and microworms immediately.

Barbs

The family of Barbs and their relatives spawn as a shoal, and the first sign that spawning is imminent is excited chasing about the

To provide a sterile 'plant' in which they will spawn, make a spawning mop from nylon knitting wool, clipped together in a bunch with a piece of lead wire. Now raise the temperature about 2 °C, and the chasing will soon become spawning in earnest, with females being driven into the mop to deposit their eggs. Remove the fish as soon as the chasing dies down. The eggs trapped in the mop will hatch within 36–48 hours, and the fry start feeding two days later, first on Infusoria, and then on microworms and brine shrimp after four days. After this first critical stage, Barbs eat most foods.

Killifish

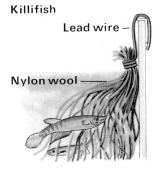

Lead wire —

Nylon wool ———

Gentle aeration of the breeding tank is necessary to satisfy the Barbs' high oxygen demands.

Egg scatterers

For small shoal fish like Danios, spawning can be even more simplified. The floor of the breeding tank is covered with a layer of glass marbles, or rounded pebbles, under a layer of water only about 10cm deep. Once more, the temperature must

Simple breeding traps

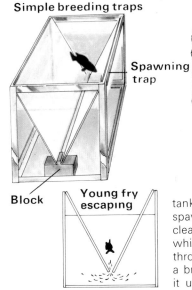

Spawning trap

Plastic netting

Block

Young fry escaping

tank. To induce actual spawning, place them in a clean, spacious tank of water which has been filtered through peat, so that it has a brownish colour, and top it up with fresh tap water.

be raised slightly, and as the shoal spawn, their eggs fall between the marbles or pebbles, where they cannot be eaten. After removal of the adults, fry are raised exactly as are the Barbs.

The White Cloud Mountain Minnows, *Tanichthys*, spawn in similar conditions but at much lower temperatures, even at normal room temperature. Most are avid egg eaters, so the tank must be well filled with spawning mops, or by fine-leaved plants like *Myriophyllum*.

Tetras and other Characins are generally difficult to spawn, being very sensitive to water conditions. They are usually spawned in pairs, in very soft acidic water, and the eggs adhere to nylon spawning mops.

Killifish

The Killis, or Egglaying Toothcarps, have some peculiar reproductive habits but will breed fairly easily in a small tank with about 15cm of water. A substrate of washed peat is desirable, and either floating plants or a spawning mop should be provided. Eggs are laid over a prolonged period, so the fry hatch at irregular intervals, and must be quickly sorted into groups of similar sized fish to avoid cannibalism. Nearly all can feed on newly hatched brine shrimp or microworms as soon as they hatch. Unlike most egg-layers, Killifish do not generally eat their eggs or young, so the parents can remain in the breeding tank until you are certain that spawning is complete. Remove them after spawning, as they may be unable to resist the temptation for long. In species such as *Aphyosemion* hatching is delayed from 10 days to as long as six months. Obviously breeding such fish is extremely specialized and requires considerable knowledge of the species involved. For some types, it will be necessary to allow eggs to dry out, still embedded in the peat substance, before they will hatch, to approximate to the conditions in the annual puddles in which the fish originally lived. You will need to know the exact species of fish you propose to breed before precise recommendations as to the breeding conditions required can be made. If in doubt, try the methods described above, and if these do not succeed, consult more specialized works for detailed advice.

Labyrinth Fish

The Labyrinth Fish, possessing accessory breathing organs, mostly breed by means of bubble nests. Nest building is preceded by prolonged courtship displays by the male fish, who will attack any other fish in the tank, so the pair must be placed in a separate breeding tank without delay. Provide adequate plants, including floating plants, to ensure that the female can escape the attentions of the male if she is not yet ready for mating, as she may otherwise be killed. The male generally builds the bubble nest, which is up to 7cm in diameter, and may rise several cm above the surface. When the female is ready to spawn, the male will attract her to his nest, literally wrap himself around her, and turn her on her back as she releases the eggs. After the pair separate, both fish collect the fertilized eggs in their mouths and spit them into the nest. At this

point the female should be removed as the male guards the nest and will attack her. The eggs hatch in 3–4 days, and the young remain in the nest for a further three days, after which the male must be removed. The young are very small-mouthed and delicate. The parent fish, being air-breathers, are not particular about water quality, but in the young, the labyrinth organ does not develop for a few days, so they need well aerated water. As they begin to breathe, fry are particularly sensitive to cold air, so the tank must be kept tightly covered to prevent chill. Feed the young fish first on Infusoria, then on the usual fry foods, bearing in mind that the Labyrinth Fish are very carnivorous, and may reject the normal dried foods. Most Labyrinth Fish demand a high temperature for breeding and rearing the young— up to 30°C. The Paradise Fish *Macropodus opercularis* is an exception, breeding at temperatures as low as 21°C. They will live and breed in an unheated tank in the average living room. Some of the larger Labyrinth fish scatter floating eggs without building a nest or caring for them in any way.

Cichlids

Breeding Cichlids is easy and very rewarding, but at the same time fraught with problems resulting from the boisterous behaviour of these fish. Cichlids pair off to breed, but will not always accept the mate you provide, resulting in fierce battles. With any type of Cichlids, it is best to buy a number of immature fish, and allow them to select mates as they mature. As the fish near sexual maturity, the males become very territorial, and having selected a suitable breeding spot will drive off all the other fish apart from the chosen mate. It is best to remove all the other fish rather than disturb the pair and risk further fighting.

The basic requirement for all Cichlids is similar, dependent on the size of the fish. A moderate sized tank with a deep bed of clean gravel and a number of stones, flowerpots, pieces of slate, etc. offers the fish a number of options for their spawning site. Don't bother about plants, as they will be speedily uprooted. Most prefer slightly acidic water, which is not too hard.

When breeding is imminent, both fish prepare the spawning site which may be a pit dug in the gravel, a piece of stone, or even the tank glass. Dwarf species tend to hide their spawn inside a flowerpot or cave.

After spawning, both parents guard the eggs and remove any which are infertile or fungused. Parents can usually be left with the fry for at least a month, by which time they are ready to spawn again. Fry hatch

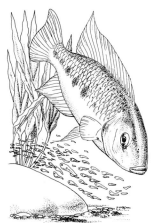

within 2–4 days, and larger types can immediately eat brine shrimp and microworms.

The recently introduced African Cichlids from Lakes Malawi and Nyasa demand rather different techniques. They need hard alkaline water, and very large stones with caves in which they can hide their eggs. Unlike most other Cichlids, the adults need algae in their diet if they are to reach breeding condition.

Discus Fish

Unless you are prepared to invest considerable time and money, it is seldom worth trying to breed the exotic Discus, *Symphysodon* sp. They demand a large tank, established mated fish, very soft acid water, and an enormous amount of patience. A number of quite unrelated fish breed in the same manner as the Cichlids, such as the catfish *Loricaria*, the Bumblebee Goby *Brachygobius xauthozona* and several species of freshwater pufferfish.

Setting up the marine aquarium

Setting up your marine aquarium is no more difficult than a freshwater tank, although there are some special requirements you will have to take into account. Be particularly careful not to let any metal come into contact with the water, as salt water is extremely corrosive, and some dissolved metals are very toxic to fish. To be on the safe side, bearing in mind the higher cost of marine fish, keep a spare pump handy, in case of failure which would mean the very quick breakdown of the organisms in the biological filter in the gravel, and equally fast fouling of the water.

Some of the equipment requirements of the marine aquarist have been discussed earlier in this book. Of these, the most important is the choice of tank. It is almost inevitable that the beginner will use a modern all-glass tank with cemented joints to avoid all possible troubles with corrosion. The only practical alternative is a tank with a plastic-coated metal frame, which is much more expensive, and not so attractive.

Setting up is exactly the same as for the freshwater tank, except that the gravel or substrate covering the biological filter needs special consideration. To maintain the correct water chemistry it helps to have a calcareous or limey substrate instead of gravel. This can be crushed limestone, shell grit or, preferably, coral sand composed of broken coral skeletons. A new type of substrate is composed of the crushed skeletons of a type of stony algae growing in the North Sea and other colder oceans. All these materials have one benefit;

▼ The Clown Triggerfish, equipped to eat coral, will chew up wiring and filters with equal enjoyment.

▼ The Archerfish enjoys nothing better than shooting down houseflies. It will also shoot out a lighted cigarette held over the tank in a darkened room.

they are porous, and in their cavities huge colonies of useful bacteria can develop, to help break down nitrogenous wastes. 8cm of substrate will provide an adequate filter bed.

Making up sea water
Next is the water. Don't skimp on this; buy synthetic salt of a reputable make, and stick to this type when topping up later. To make up your sea water you will need a large plastic container, like a dustbin—obviously it must be very clean. Detailed instructions will be supplied with your pack of salt, but the following general points will also apply. Mix the salt with ordinary tap water, stirring thoroughly with a wooden or plastic stirrer until it has all dissolved. You will have to let the solution stand for 24 hours to allow chlorine to escape, and to be on the safe side, you may care to aerate the water to speed up the process. Syphon the water into the tank to avoid disturbing the filter.

Now add the heater, thermostat, thermometer, and external filter if used, as recommended for setting up the freshwater tank. Switch on, and leave overnight for the temperature to stabilize.

Decoration
Your fish will require hiding

▶ Beware the large mouth and rapid growth of the Grouper. It could prove expensive if kept with smaller tankmates.

places, and the tank needs some decoration, and for the marine tank, coral is the only safe material to use. Use rock only if you are absolutely sure of its chemical composition, and know it to be non-toxic. You can buy coral from aquarists and from dealers who supply it as a household decoration. Even if you have had a cherished piece of coral for many years, it will still contain sufficient organic remains to produce huge quantities of bacteria in a few days, so it will need very careful cleaning. The same goes for coral from a dealer, supposedly already clean. Place your coral in a plastic bucket, and cover it with a 5% solution of caustic soda (handle with care) or with a strong solution of domestic bleach. Leave for at least 24 hours, then wash thoroughly, and soak in sea water for a week before use.

Remember that marine fish are aggressive, and provide adequate hiding places for the shyer types. Cement your coral together or to the tank sides with silicone aquarium sealant.

Introducing the fish
Your tank is now ready for its first fish, and the golden rule is 'Don't be over ambitious'. The filter bed in your new tank is almost sterile, and will be unable to break down nitrite which soon accumulates in the water. What you must do is to mature the filter bed. This can be done in two ways. A handful of substrate from a well-stocked dealer's tank can be stirred into your own tank. This seeds your own substrate with millions of beneficial bacteria. Now add one or two small fish to produce the nitrites which the bacteria need. Damselfish are the obvious choice,

being cheap, tough, and above all, tolerant of the drastic changes in water chemistry which are going to take place over the next few weeks. *Scatophagus* and *Monodactylus*, which are often kept in freshwater, live in polluted harbours and are equally tolerant of changes in water conditions (but make sure they are already acclimatized to sea water). Feeding on the fishes' urine, droppings, and broken-down food particles, the bacteria multiply enormously. If you can monitor nitrate and nitrite levels with a test kit, you will see these rise to very high levels after

▼ The Lionfish, *Pterois volitans* is a beautiful and easily kept fish, but beware of its poisonous spines.

a couple of weeks, then drop to an acceptable level after about a month as the bacteria get to work. They need plentiful oxygen, so keep the air pump working continuously, otherwise the useful bacteria will die and be replaced by some dangerous types.

When you decide to add more fish, exercise caution. If you add too many, you may overload the bacterial filter. By now your Damselfish will be thoroughly established and will have claimed the best spots in the tank as their personal domain. They will inevitably harrass any new arrivals, so for your next purchase, try and get a fish which can look after itself, like a Tang or a Wrasse. Add new fish a few at a time, preferably just after feeding the original inhabi-

tants, to distract their attention. Moving the coral or adding fresh coral shelters also disrupts the territorial inclinations of the toughest fish; all the tankmates now have to find a new home.

Food
Feeding is a critical time, especially for new fish. In theory, the fish you buy will have been kept for a while in a dealer's tank, and should have been weaned onto artificial or dead foods. Unfortunately, some were probably caught only a few days before, so you will have to tempt them to eat with brine shrimp, freeze-dried foods, pieces of fish, or any titbit which arouses their interest. Tangs and some other species need vegetable food such as shredded lettuce, which forms an es-

sential part of their diet. Deep-frozen foods are extremely useful, and pieces can be shaved off from a block of food, and dropped into the tank, where the fish eat fragments as they thaw. It is doubly important to prevent uneaten food fragments from decaying on the tank bottom, so do not overfeed. Some freeze-dried foods can be pressed onto the tank glass, where they adhere while the fish pick at them, and so will not be wasted. Don't neglect the shyer fish, such as the Royal Gramma, which may be kept away from food by bolder species. You may need to drop food near their hiding place to make sure they get their fair share.

Sickness

Disease is an ever-present problem, and *Oodinium* is the worst threat. It resembles the freshwater White Spot Disease in its life cycle, although the cysts forming on the fish are smaller. Treatment of the water with a proprietary cure containing copper is the best remedy, although this cannot be used in tanks containing invertebrates such as anemones, shrimps, or crabs, which are very sensitive to dissolved metals. Detailed instructions are supplied with the drug, and should be followed exactly. Treatment must be continued for several days, and a partial water change is recommended once the disease is fully controlled. Other diseases of marine fish need specialized diagnosis and treatment. See the reading list on p.88 for useful sources of further information.

Cleaning and hygiene

The marine tank is kept clean and hygienic in exactly the same way as the freshwater tank, although even more scrupulous care is needed, especially in removing mulm (fish excreta and other solid wastes) and uneaten food.

Once a month, you will need to change about quarter of the water, syphoning it off in the usual way. Make up more water, using your standard salt mix, but before adding it to the tank, check its salinity using a hydrometer. This is a floating glass tube which will tell you the specific gravity (SG) of the water, which must be the same for both the tank and the water used for topping up. Periodic checks of the tank SG should also be made. Water is lost through evaporation, and must be replaced with *fresh* water to bring the SG back to its correct reading, which varies with temperature, and can be read off on a chart supplied with the hydrometer. In the average marine tank, the temperatures may range between 21–27°C. pH can sometimes vary in a marine tank, but if coral sand or other calcareous substrates are used, will naturally hover around the optimum 7.5–8.3. If ever you have recurring losses which are otherwise inexplicable, buy a pH test kit and check.

Algae and invertebrates

Marine algae for the aquarium are not the familiar brown seaweeds, but smaller creeping plants with fern-like fronds. They are rather difficult to get established, and, if they do not thrive, will decay at an alarming rate. Invertebrates like anemones are very attractive, especially if they make a home for Clownfish, which swim inside the grasp of their poisonous tentacles with impunity. Unfortunately, these large anemones are plankton feeders, and tend to deteriorate slowly in the aquarium, unless special arrangements are made for feeding them. Invertebrates such as crabs and shrimps are not easy to keep, often being attacked by the fish, although small hermit crabs do make useful scavengers. Living rock or live coral is often offered for sale, complete with all its attached worms, sponges, and other forms of life. It is very difficult to keep these delicate organisms healthy, and Butterfly fish are very fond of eating the coral polyps.

Hygiene and main- tenance

Within a couple of months of being set up, your aquarium will have stabilized itself. Cloudy water, overgrowths of algae, and similar problems should have passed, and you will be able to settle down to the minimal routine maintenance necessary to keep the tank attractive and the fish and plants looking healthy. Alterations to your aquarium habitat need extra care; the addition of new fish, or the use of a different type of food can sometimes cause problems. In general, tank maintenance is a matter of commonsense, and serious problems only arise as a result of overcrowding or overfeeding.

Use your air pump to power convenient gadgets such as the aquarium 'vacuum cleaner'.

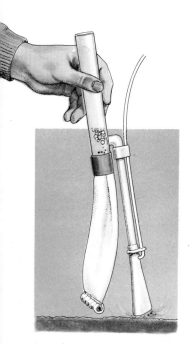

The standard tool for keeping the tank floor clean of mulm is the siphon. The easiest siphon to use is a simple length of plastic hose, about 1cm internal diameter, and 1m in length. Place one end in the tank, and suck the other end until water has nearly reached your mouth (use clear plastic tubing!). Now quickly lower the end into a bucket stood on the floor, and a jet of water will flow. Manoeuvre the end in the tank so the water draws off all the mulm, which will have collected in the tank corners, and in hollows in the gravel. Take care not to siphon up the gravel as well as the mulm. You can avoid this problem, and the risk of getting a mouthful of bacteria-laden water, by using an automatic siphon, a gadget which starts the water flowing when you submerge it in the tank. A better method is to use a 'vacuum cleaner', powered by your air pump, which collects the

Change $\frac{1}{3}$ of the tank water every 2 months.

mulm in a cloth bag, and does not remove any water. These devices churn up the top layer of the gravel, without the risk of sucking it up, and so remove particles of uneaten food.

Water change

The nitrogen cycle, discussed on p.11, means that there will be a steady build-up of potentially harmful chemicals in the water; too much for the plants to neutralize. If you remove all the mulm from the tank, the problem will be minimized, for it is bacterial decay of the mulm which releases most of the nitrite into the water. Use of an outside

Use a *nylon* scourer to remove algae from glass.

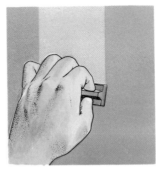

Plastic scrapers are also available.

Sever runners before transplanting.

filter has the same effect, but you must change the filter medium regularly or the bacterial breakdown will occur in the filter, and pass harmful nitrogenous substances back into the tank.

Unless you have deliberately set up artificially altered water conditions for a particular type of fish, it is simplest to avoid all water chemistry problems by replacing about one-third of the water every two months. In practice, this is most conveniently done when water is being siphoned off for cleaning. Replace with normal tap water, which must be at *exactly* the same temperature as the tank water. In this small amount, chlorinated tap water will not harm the fish, and can be used immediately. Don't tip water in from a bucket or the surge will uproot the plants and seriously disturb sensitive fish. It is best to siphon topping-up water into the tank, from a plastic

bucket which must be stood on a surface higher than the water level in the tank— otherwise the siphon will not flow. If this is inconvenient, rig up an air lift to carry water up into the tank, using the air-lift mechanism from an outside filter. You will probably find the small taps and T-piece connectors available from stockists to be useful for these purposes; a tap is very handy to stop water siphoning *back* down the tubing and all over the floor.

Trimming plants
Your aquarium will probably contain a mixture of rapidly-growing bunch plants, and the slower-growing decorative plants like *Cryptocoryne*, which are easily 'swamped' and strangled by the more vigorously growing types. Keep pinching-out the growing tips of the bunch plants. This will make them branch and become bushier. The lengths you pinch off

can be replanted to make new clumps. Often the original plants will have deteriorated, and are best replaced with healthy growths from the tips, which take root and grow very rapidly. In all types of plant, some leaves naturally die off, and must be cut off with scissors and removed before they can decay. Snail attacks often lead to an entire leaf rotting off, so any snails you can see should be removed and destroyed. If you have carefully arranged your tank layout so that areas of bare gravel are bounded by clumps of plants, you may need to control the spread of plants by runners growing through the gravel. Don't attempt to pull these out; you will uproot the plant, and it is difficult to push all the roots back under the gravel. Instead, run a sharp knife or razor blade through the gravel to sever them without disturbing the other plants.

Problems

Considering the exotic origins of most aquarium fish, problems are surprisingly few. Even for marine fish, difficulties become less as more knowledge of their requirements is gained. With commonsense and prudence, no disaster need ever happen to your fish, although a certain number must inevitably die each year through natural causes. But because accidents and the unexpected can happen, it is always wise to keep a cheap plastic tank available in case of emergency; it can also be used as a quarantine tank for when you buy new fish.

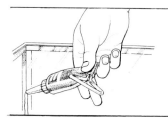

Leaks

Leaks are the most worrying problem of all for the beginner. A complete cure can be effected by emptying the tank, keeping fish and plants in your spare plastic tank. Dry the inside scrupulously, then run a thin fillet of silicone aquarium adhesive around the inside seams. Allow to cure for at least 48 hours before replacing the fish.

Algae

Algae grows naturally in the aquarium, and is especially common in the newly set-up tank. If the lighting is too strong, an overgrowth of algae will occur. Cut down the light by partly obscuring the lamp with a piece of card or paper — not too much or the algae will die quickly and pollute the water. Experiment until the light is sufficient for healthy plant growth, but does not cause much algae growth.

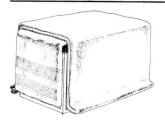

Power cuts

Like leaks, power cuts always seem more worrying than they need be. In practice, it takes a good while for a tank to cool off completely, and if you wrap it entirely in blankets, the fish will be safe for several hours. For longer periods, as a last resort, top up with hot water from the kettle, stirring it in gently. Special plugs for freezers can be obtained which buzz if there is a fault in your own power supply.

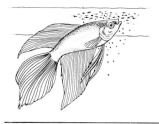

Overfeeding

The golden rule is: feed only the amount of food that the fish will consume in five minutes. If you see black gravel developing, fungus growths in the mulm, or worse still foul-smelling bubbles on the surface, siphon off uneaten food and change two-thirds of the water, or you will have an expensive and smelly disaster on your hands. Starve the fish for a few days and try to use more live foods.

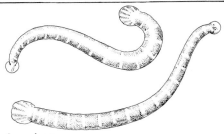

Snails

Snails are a mixed blessing in the tank. Some people keep them to remove algae from the glass; a task much better done with a hand scraper. Unfortunately, snails breed very fast, and soon turn their attention to the plants. Pick unwanted snails out by hand, or leave a lettuce leaf in the tank overnight as bait to attract them.

Leeches

Leeches are common in the aquarium, but being nocturnal, are seldom seen. They look like small earthworms, and either glide about the tank bottom, or swim with an undulating motion. Once in the tank, they are almost impossible to eradicate, short of sterilizing all the gravel by heat and starting again.

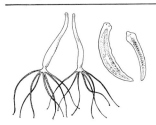

Planaria and Hydra

In a long-established tank you will often see tiny 1–3mm Planaria gliding about on the glass when you switch the lights on. You may also find Hydra, like tiny sea anemones about 1cm long. Neither cause serious problems, but they can look unsightly. They are very difficult to eradicate, and as they seldom cause difficulties it is probably not worth using chemicals to try and control them.

Chills

Cold affects tropical fish in subtle ways. Disease outbreaks often follow a chill, when the weakened fish become susceptible to infections already present in the tank. But some fish react by 'shimmying'; a peculiar wobbling movement, when the fish seems to be swimming without actually going anywhere. Raise temperature immediately to 1–2°C above the usual tank temperature and watch out for a possible outbreak of White Spot disease.

Fumes.

Most substances in the air dissolve in water, and many are toxic to the fish. Tobacco smoke, and particularly fumes from enamel paint are bad for fish, and should be minimized by switching *off* the air pump whenever you consider the risk to be high. If necessary, you can lead the air intake pipe from the pump out into unpolluted air. Remove oily films from the water surface by floating a layer of absorbent paper in the tank for a few minutes.

Diseases

Most types of disease are infectious, and caused by either bacteria or, more usually, by microscopic animals or fungi. These disease organisms are often present in the tank, but do not cause problems unless some change in conditions weakens the fish, who normally possess some immunity to them. The other types of disease are introduced with imported wild fish, and are often quite difficult to eradicate. If any fish fails to respond to treatment, it is best to kill it painlessly by throwing it very hard against a solid surface, rather than allowing it to continue suffering and possibly infect the whole tank.

Ichthyophthirius
(White Spot or Ich)

The greatest scourge of the freshwater tropical aquarium, caused by protozoan parasites which cause raised white cysts on the surface of the fish, about 0.5–1mm in diameter. The disease is often introduced with newly purchased stock, and the spots begin to appear on the other fish after a few days. The first sign is that the fish begin to scratch themselves against rocks and plants, and the tell-tale white spots appear soon after. They seem to clear spontaneously in a few days, but during this period, the parasites are multiplying in the gravel, and soon swarm out to infect the fish in even greater numbers. White Spot will speedily prove fatal to all the fish if not treated with a proprietary cure. Some brands are not suitable for use in a planted tank, and the fish may have to be transferred to an unplanted tank for treatment. After a few days without any suitable host on which to settle, the remaining parasites will starve to death, and the tank can be used again.

Saprolegnia

Injured or weakened fish are often attacked by Saprolegnia fungus, which grows like cotton-wool on the injured part. It is potentially fatal, but responds to treatment, which consists of a daily swabbing of the affected area with 5% methylene blue solution.

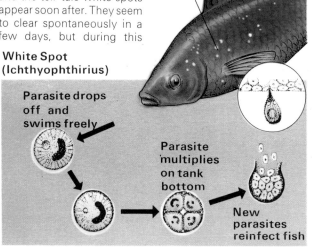

White cysts on fish

White Spot (Ichthyophthirius)

Parasite drops off and swims freely

Parasite multiplies on tank bottom

New parasites reinfect fish

Saprolegnia

Popeyes

Bulging eyes are symptoms of various diseases, and are difficult to cure. Frequently, parasitic flukes are the cause, brought in with wild fish. The condition is seldom infectious, and does not always trouble the affected fish, so it is not usually worth treating.

Dropsy

Occasionally a fish will be found to look swollen, with the scales sticking out at an angle. This too can be a symptom of various diseases, and any fish suffering from it should be destroyed immediately, as the condition is generally incurable.

Oodinium

(Velvet, Saltwater Ich)
Oodinium disease often attacks freshwater fish after a chill. It appears as a fine dusting of white spots, much smaller than those of the common White Spot Disease. It has a similar life cycle to White Spot, but unfortunately the parasites can survive for a long while away from a fish host, so it is difficult to eradicate com-

Dropsy

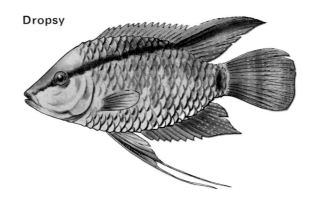

pletely once it has appeared. Not only must the fish be removed and treated with a proprietary cure in a separate tank, but the gravel and plants must be rinsed in potassium permanganate solution before being reused.

In the marine tank, a different species of Oodinium is the commonest cause of disease, and can bring heavy losses. Treat with a proprietary cure containing copper sulphate, and remember that copper is highly toxic to invertebrates, so remove these first.

Neon Disease

This disease attacks the Neon Tetra and its close relatives, appearing as whitish speckles which spread rapidly from fish to fish. It is difficult to cure, but may respond if the fish are kept in strong solutions of a proprietary mixture of methylene blue and acroflavin.

Fin Rot

Damaged fins often suffer from bacterial attack, which can eventually kill the fish. The disease usually responds to regular swabbing with 5% methylene blue solution.

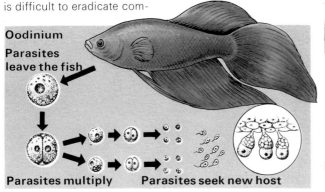

Oodinium

Parasites leave the fish

Parasites multiply **Parasites seek new host**

Fin and Tail Rot

Guide to freshwater fish

N.B. Number in brackets refers to illustration.

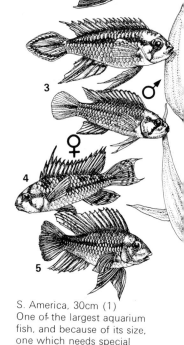

1 ♂

2

3 ♂

♀

4

5

CICHLIDS

Of the hundreds of species of Cichlids, only a few are suitable for the average aquarium, such as the Angelfish and some of the dwarf species. The larger types, with few exceptions, are voracious carnivores and are unsuitable for the community tank. They must be kept in special Cichlid tanks, where they cannot damage their tankmates. Recently they have become popular with the introduction of a whole range of hitherto unknown types from Lakes Nyasa and Tanganyika in East Africa. These small Cichlids all live in deep water, which is extremely hard and alkaline. Their colours and markings rival those of marine fish, and, as they seem to breed quite easily, they will be lastingly popular. Unlike most other cichlids, fish of different species can generally be mixed without trouble, as in their natural habitat they live in such mixed colonies. Most of them need some algae in their diet, and they are generally mouthbrooders. Even apparently peaceful Cichlids need careful watching in the aquarium, as they are quite capable of turning murderous for no apparent reason.

Aequidens latifrons
(Blue Acara)
S. America, 15cm (2)
An early favourite, with subdued but attractive colours. Extremely hardy, and relatively peaceful for such a large fish. Easy to breed, and recommended for the beginner.

Apistogramma agassizi
S. America, up to 7cm, female smaller (3)
Like its relatives, this dwarf Cichlid is rather secretive, and is aggressive against its own kind. All the *Apistogramma* species hide their eggs in small caves or flowerpots, the female guarding the young and usually driving her mate away.

Apistogramma borelli
S. America, up to 6cm, female smaller (4)
Less common than the preceding species. Breeds as *A. agassizi.*

Apistogramma reitzigi
S. America, up to 5cm, female smaller (5)
Colours and shape less attractive than the preceding species, but more peaceful in the community tank.

Astronotus ocellatus
(Oscar, Velvet Cichlid, Marbled Cichlid)
S. America, 30cm (1)
One of the largest aquarium fish, and because of its size, one which needs special treatment. Young fish are dark brown, with a beautiful marbled pattern. Adults have an olive-brown colouration, with a number of bright orange spots near the tail. These fish grow

very rapidly, feeding on worms, smaller fish, and chunks of meat. They appear to be intelligent, will feed from the hand and seem to recognize their owner. Not to be trusted with other fish, even when young.

Cichlasoma biocellatum
(Jack Dempsey)
S. America, up to 20cm (7)
This large Cichlid is very bad news for any other fish unfortunate enough to share its tank. Its beautiful colouration makes up for its bad temperament.

Cichlasoma cyanoguttatum
(Texas Cichlid, Rio Grande Perch)
Mexico and Texas, 30cm (11)
Similar in temperament and appearance to *C. biocellatum*, but with light blue mottling. Very hardy and easy to breed,

this fish prefers cooler water than most tropical fish.

Cichlasoma festivum
S. America, 15cm (6)
Although the genus *Cichlasoma* contains some very pugnacious fish, *C. festivum* is comparatively mild-mannered and retiring. It keeps in mid-water, and is rather shy and difficult to breed. Suitable for keeping in a community tank with large fish, *C. festivum* prefers some algae in its diet.

Cichlasoma meeki
(Firemouth)
Central and S. America, 15cm (10)
A large and spectacular fish which develops a beautiful fiery colour when in breeding condition. It breeds very easily, and the parents usually raise

their young without problems. Not to be trusted with any but the largest tankmates.

Haplochromis burtoni
E. Africa, 10cm (13)
A mouthbrooder with a good temperament. Colours are predominantly blue, with prominent 'egg spots' on the anal fin.

Haplochromis moorii
Lake Nyasa, 20 cm (9)
One of the new E. African Cichlids, of a brilliant blue colour. Males and females both develop a hump on their foreheads. Likes foraging for small particles of food, and prefers a sandy bottom in which it can dig.

Haplochromis multicolor
(Egyptian Mouthbrooder)
E. Africa, 7cm (8)

Quiet and inoffensive Cichlid which is suitable for the community tank. Colours are subdued but attractive, and the fish breeds very easily, proving an excellent parent.

Julidochromis ornatus
(Golden Julie)
Lake Tanganyika, 7cm (12)
One of the aristocrats of the new African Cichlids. Rather expensive and quite scrappy, so best kept as a mated pair in a separate tank. As with other E. African cichlids, it prefers hard, alkaline water.

Labeotropheus trewavasae
Lake Nyasa, 12cm (14)
Another African species with an attractive pale blue colouration, and a reddish dorsal fin.

Nannacara anomala
(Golden-eyed Dwarf Cichlid)
S. America, 7cm (16)
This quiet and inoffensive Dwarf Cichlid is ideal for the community tank.

Nannochromis nudiceps
Congo, 7cm (15)
A W. African Dwarf Cichlid with predominantly green colouring and a pink blotch covering the abdomen. Prefers soft acid water, unlike the E. African types. Keep at temperatures a few degrees higher than other Cichlids.

Pelmatochromis pulcher
(incorrectly known as
P. kribensis)
Nigeria, 7cm (17)
A very popular dwarf Cichlid which prefers soft water, and extra warmth, and often breeds in the community tank. Digs less than most other Cichlids, and will often nibble at filamentous algae.

Pelmatochromis subocellatus
(Eye Spot Cichlid)
W. Africa, 10cm (18)
Very similar to the preceding species, but has marbling on the tail and dorsal fin, instead of the 'eye spots' of
P. pulcher.

Pseudotropheus auratus
Lake Nyasa, 11cm (23)
Both sexes are an attractive yellow, with white and brown longitudinal stripes, except that the dominant male in breeding colouration assumes a darker, steel-blue colouring. Will tolerate other species of Nyasa Cichlids in the same tank.

Pseudotropheus elongatus
Lake Nyasa, 12cm (21)
An elongated E. African Cichlid adapted to browsing on algae covering the rocks. Male and female are difficult to distinguish, the female being slightly paler in colour.

Pseudotropheus novemfasciatus
Lake Nyasa, 10cm (20)
A small, blunt-headed species of an attractive chestnut-brown colour. Rather pugnacious.

Pseudotropheus tropheops
Lake Nyasa, 12cm (22)
Another of the Nyasa group, in which males and females

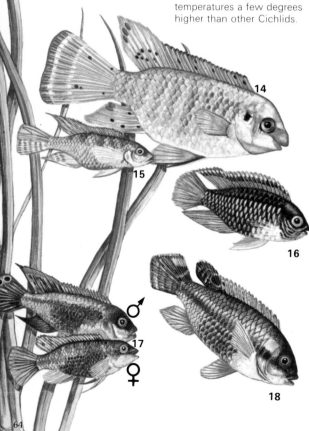

14

15

16

♂

17

♀

18

have quite different colouration

Pseudotropheus zebra
Lake Nyasa, 15cm (24)
A large and aggressive Nyasa Cichlid which grazes on algae. It is extremely variable in colour, males being predominantly blue, while many females have orange and black blotches.

Pterophyllum scalare
(Angelfish)
S. America, 15cm (19)
Too well known to need description; most of the Cichlid viciousness has been bred out of the Angelfish, although it will always snap up fish small enough to be swallowed whole. Grows much larger than most people realize.

Symphysodon aequifasciata
(Discus) S. America, 13cm (26)
Symphysodon discus
(Discus) S. America, 20cm (25)
These two species, the aristocrats of the freshwater aquarium, are so similar as to be treated in the same way. They are very delicate and temperamental, being intolerant of any form of pollution, and susceptible to disease. Keep in soft water in a tank of their own, and disturb the fish as little as possible.

Discus are finicky feeders, but most will eat freeze-dried Tubifex. If Discus do breed, don't remove eggs from the parents' care, as the young feed on their body slime for the first few days.

Tropheus duboisi
Lake Tanganyika, 7cm (28)
Adults of this fish are very dark, with a broad transverse reddish stripe, but juveniles

65

are exceptionally beautiful, being black with a mottling of white spots.

Tropheus moorei

(Moorish Cichlid)
Lake Tanganyika, 10cm (27)
Similar to the above, but adults have a brilliant red band in the dorsal fin above the body stripe. Needs a large tank for swimming space. Intolerant of its own species but quite harmless to other Cichlids. Grazes on algae. Highly recommended.

LOACHES AND SHARKS

Although these two groups of fish are only distantly related, it is convenient to discuss them and some other types together, as they are similar in habit and appearance. Few if any have been bred in the aquarium.

Loaches are fish of fast-flowing waters, but can take in extra oxygen by swallowing bubbles of air.

So-called Sharks, which are

actually Cyprinids, closely related to the Barbs and Rasboras, generally inhabit larger rivers, but are very powerful swimmers, grazing off algae with their tough leathery lips.

Both types of fish are rather secretive and partly nocturnal. They will only thrive if given plenty of hiding places, and, if they feel secure, will lose much of their shyness. They are given to dashing rapidly about the tank if frightened, and need a reasonable amount of swimming space.

Loaches and sharks are good community fish, sometimes being aggressive with their own kind.

LOACHES

Loaches are excellent aquarium scavengers. Their undershot mouth is equipped with short barbels with which they can detect food particles, and they dig vigorously into the gravel to extract Tubifex worms, of which they are particularly fond. In general, they create less mess than Catfish, and are not so likely to uproot the plants. Loaches have a long, curved spine beneath each eye, which is normally retracted, but which they raise when frightened. Take care when handling them in a net, as the spine can cause an unpleasant cut, and will become entangled in the mesh of the net.

These fish have the disturbing habit of resting on the gravel, lying flat on their sides, which can be most disconcerting with a newly purchased fish. As they have no scales, they are particularly susceptible to skin diseases.

Acanthophthalmus kuhlii
(Coolie Loach)
Indonesia, 8cm (41)

This worm-like loach is typical of a number of similar species, having indigo bands about a fleshy pink body. These fish are small, shy, and secretive, but search continuously for scraps of food. Highly recommended for the community tank, but make sure other fish are not big enough to eat them.

Acanthophthalmus semicinctus
(Half-banded Coolie) Indonesia, 8cm (40)
As above, and usually sold as *A. kuhlii*. Stripes are less distinct and end at the mid-line.

Botia horae
(Skunk Loach) S.E. Asia, 10cm (32)
A small, shy, pink-coloured species which is very peaceful. It prefers cooler temperatures and harder water than the other species of Botia.

Botia hymenophysa
(Tiger Loach) S.E. Asia, up to 21cm (30)
Handsomely striped, but very shy and seldom visible in the tank. A very powerful swimmer.

Botia macracanthus
(Clown Loach) Sumatra and Borneo, up to 30cm (31)
One of the most popular and most expensive of the loaches, because of its brilliant colouration. Clown Loach swim in schools, and once established, are quite hardy. Clown Loach do not reach their full size in aquaria, seldom exceeding 12cm in length. This and the other species of *Botia* prefer soft, acid water, and a fairly high temperature of 24–28°C.

Botia modesta
S.E. Asia, 10cm (33)
Resembles the previous species in its requirements. Subdued bluish colours, but less shy than most loaches and quite active by day.

Botia sidthimunki
(Dwarf Loach) Thailand, 3.5cm (34)
This little fish does best in shoals. Unlike most other Loaches, it swims clear of the tank bottom, and is not shy. Highly recommended.

SHARKS AND RELATED TYPES

Balantiocheilus melanopterus
(Silver Shark) Indonesia, 35cm (29)
This magnificent fish obviously requires a large tank, and robust tankmates. It is capable of tremendous leaps, so the tank must be kept well covered. Eats anything, including the plants, and prefers to swim in schools.

Epalzeorhynchus kallopterus
(Flying Fox) Borneo and Sumatra, 14cm (35)
An attractively marked fish which eats algae and is an effective scavenger. Inactive for much of the time, but can move very fast when frightened. One of the few fish which will eat Planarians. Needs plenty of cover.

Gyrinocheilus aymonieri
(Sucking Loach, Algae Eater) Thailand, up to 25cm, usually much smaller (36)
This fish is not a Loach at all, but is a relative of the Barbs. It is the most effective eater of algae, and cleans the leaves and glass incessantly. Colours are subdued. Quiet and

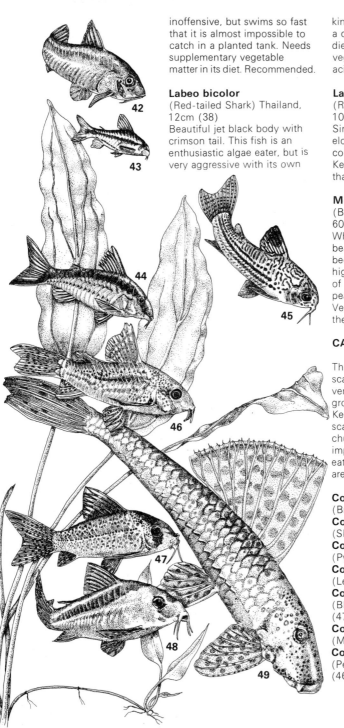

inoffensive, but swims so fast that it is almost impossible to catch in a planted tank. Needs supplementary vegetable matter in its diet. Recommended.

Labeo bicolor
(Red-tailed Shark) Thailand, 12cm (38)
Beautiful jet black body with crimson tail. This fish is an enthusiastic algae eater, but is very aggressive with its own kind, and is best kept singly in a community tank. Needs its diet supplemented with vegetable matter. Prefers soft acid water.

Labeo frenatus
(Red-finned Shark) S.E. Asia 10cm (37)
Similar to above, but more elongated and less strikingly coloured, with reddish fins. Keeps to middle water rather than the tank bottom.

Morulius chrysophekadion
(Black Shark) Thailand 60cm (39)
When small, this fish is a beautiful velvety black, which becomes lighter with bronze highlights as it grows. In spite of its potential size, very peaceful and not at all shy. Very hardy and easily kept in the largest tanks.

CATFISH

The most satisfactory scavengers of all, Catfish are very hardy, although some grow to a disconcerting size. Keep their tank clean, as their scavenging will otherwise churn up the sediment into an impenetrable murk. Most will eat anything, and some species are voracious predators.

Corydoras aeneus
(Bronze Catfish) 5cm (42)
Corydoras arcuatus
(Skunk Catfish) 5cm (44)
Corydoras hastatus
(Pygmy Catfish) 3cm (43)
Corydoras julii
(Leopard Catfish) 6cm (45)
Corydoras melanistius
(Black-spotted Catfish) 6cm (47)
Corydoras myersi
(Myer's Catfish) 6cm (48)
Corydoras paleatus
(Peppered Corydoras) 7cm (46)

All these species are from S. America.
With the single exception of *C. hastatus*, which lives more in the middle waters, all these armoured Catfish are bottom-livers. All swim in shoals, even of mixed species, and are totally inoffensive to other fish, secure in their body armour. These Catfish need hard water to allow their bony armour to develop properly. They eat anything, and some will breed easily, fastening their eggs to stones rather like Cichlids, although they do not care for eggs or young.

Hypostomus species
(Sucker Catfish) S. America, up to 30 cm (49)
Several species of *Hypostomus*, *Plecostomus* and *Xenocara* are imported. All have similar habits and appearance, and some grow large. They have enormous sucking mouths with which they clean tank glass, stones, and leaves of algae. They all need supplementary greenstuff in their diet. Robust and strong swimmers, which are peaceable, but quite capable of defending themselves from aggressive fish—even some large Cichlids.

Kryptopterus bicirrhis
(Glass Catfish) S.E. Asia 10 cm (53)
Deceptively fragile-looking fish which is totally transparent, with all the internal organs visible. Will thrive only in a shoal, living in mid-water, and eating only live foods.

Loricaria filamentosa
(Whiptail Catfish) S. America, 12cm (54)
Peaceful fish with a sucker mouth, feeding mostly on algae. Habits and appearance like that of *Hypostomus*, but smaller and more manageable. Breeds in the aquarium very like a Cichlid. Excellent fish for the community tank, hardy and long-living.

Otocinclus flexilis
(La Plata) 5cm (52, 55)
A small industrious species which spends much of its time in the upper part of the tank, even swimming upside down to clean the undersides of floating leaves. Breeds erratically, guarding its eggs, but the fry are very difficult to raise.

Pimelodus clarias
S. America, up to 20cm (56)
This species is typical of a number of S. American Catfish often imported. All are attractively marked, and have very long barbels. They are also all voracious predators, and not to be trusted with smaller fish. They do not scavenge, but prefer pieces of meat or earthworms as their diet. Other similar types are *Pimelodella*, *Microglanis*, and *Sorubim*.

Synodontis angelicus
(Polkadot Catfish) Zaire, up to 20cm (51)
Small specimens are attractively marked with white spots on a purplish body, becoming more subdued as they age. A retiring and peaceful shoaling fish, which eats anything.

Uncommon and rather expensive, but well worth looking out for. They like soft, acid water, and a minimum temperature of 20°C. Not yet bred in captivity.

Synodontis nigriventris
Central Africa, 6cm (50)
This little Catfish spends most of its time upside down, and consequently the belly is darker than its back, to maintain the usual fish camouflage effect. Eats anything, and is constantly on the move throughout the whole tank.

BARBS
Barbs are a popular and robust group of fish, needing plenty of swimming space, and preferring soft acid water. Most spawn quite easily.

Barbus conchonius
(Rosy Barb) India and Bangladesh, 12cm (60)
A very common and hardy fish, only seen at its best in breeding colours, when the male is flushed with a brilliant rose-pink. It spawns easily.

Barbus nigrofasciatus
(Nigger Barb, Black Ruby, Purple-Hearted Barb) Sri Lanka, 5cm (57)
Magnificent and deservedly popular aquarium fish, easily bred. Kept in shoals, it will remain more or less constantly in its breeding colours. Like other barbs it is omnivorous.

Barbus oligolepis
(Checker Barb) Sumatra, 5cm (58)
This barb is less spectacularly marked than other species, and also less boisterous. It likes to shoal, keeping close to the bottom and spawns very readily.

Barbus 'schuberti'
(Golden Barb) 10cm (62)
This barb exists only in captivity, being a fertile hybrid with obscure ancestry. It is very hardy and easily bred.

Barbus schwanenfeldi
(Tinsel or Tinfoil Barb) S.E. Asia, 32cm (64)
A big, deep-bodied barb, suitable only for the largest tanks, but very attractive and worth keeping. It swims fast and leaps prodigously, and its colours are best seen in a small shoal. The Tinsel Barb is omnivorous, and an effective argument for the use of plastic plants, as it will graze the natural type down to stumps within a few hours.

Barbus tetrazona
(Tiger Barb) S.E. Asia, 7cm (59)
The most popular aquarium Barb, this is an active schooling fish. Needs extra care to spawn, but is hardy and cheap. Rather aggressive, it will nip at the flowing fins of Angelfish and other slow-moving tankmates.

Barbus titteya
(Cherry Barb) 5cm, Sri Lanka (61)
One of the smallest Barbs, this is a beautiful pink with longitudinal stripes. It thrives best in shoals, kept with other small fish. Males are quarrelsome with each other, but otherwise very shy and peaceful. Spawns readily, but is not very prolific.

DANIOS
A group of small surface-dwelling fish which are very hardy and easy to breed. They require adequate swimming space and a low temperature of about 23°C.

Brachydanio albolineatus
(Pearl Danio) India and
Sumatra 5.5cm (63)
Fast-moving shoaling fish with a subtle, pearlish-pink colouration. One of the easiest egg-layers to breed.

Brachydanio 'frankei'
(Leopard Danio) S. Asia 5 cm (66)
Possibly a mutant of *B. rerio*, with the stripes broken up into blue blotches. Equally easy to care for and to breed.

Brachydanio nigrofasciatus
(Spotted Danio) Burma, 4cm (65)
Smaller and a little more delicate than *B. rerio*, the Spotted Danio is less of a shoaling fish. It is generally shy and inoffensive, spending much of the time sheltering among the plants.

Brachydanio rerio
(Zebrafish) India, 4.5cm (67)
The popular Zebrafish is one of the oldest tropical aquarium fish. Its familiar longitudinal blue stripes make a striking picture when kept, as it always should be, in a sizeable shoal. It eats anything and is completely peaceable.

Danio malabaricus
(Giant Danio) India and Sri Lanka, 12cm (68)
A larger and more robust fish than the Zebrafish and its relatives, but just as peaceful and easily spawned. When kept in a large shoal, it is very attractive.

RASBORAS

Rasbora heteromorpha
(Harlequin Fish) S.E. Asia, 4.5cm (72)
Fast-moving shoaling fish with attractive pink colouring, and a dark triangle on the side. Needs soft acid water to develop its best colouring, and is difficult to breed.

57

58 ♂ ♀

59

60 ♂ ♀

61

62

63

64

65

66

67

68

69

70

71

72

Rasbora trilineata
(Scissor-Tail) Malaysia, 12cm
(71)

Slim and elegant fish with distinctive tail markings which give it its popular name. It has a ghost-like appearance when swimming in a shoal because of its glassy and semi-transparent body. Active, and needs a reasonable amount of swimming space.

Rasbora maculata
(Pygmy Rasbora) Malaysia and Sumatra 2.5cm (70)
One of the smallest aquarium fish, this Rasbora is a quiet and shy fish which does best when kept in shoal with its own kind.

Tanichthys albonubes
(White Cloud Mountain Minnow) China, 4cm (69)
An old favourite, which looks rather drab when compared with some more recent introductions. One of the

hardiest fish for beginners, it will thrive in water temperatures of 16–22°C, doing best at around 20°C. It's ability to withstand lower temperatures means that it can be kept in outdoor pools during summer. Easily bred, and eats anything. Colours appear to be deteriorating, probably due to too much inbreeding.

TETRAS

The Tetras are a major group of Characins, and comprise the bulk of all freshwater tropical aquarium fish. Most are small and fairly peaceful, and nearly all prefer soft, acid water, which is essential when attempting to breed them. Many of the 'standard' tropical fish belong to this group.

Anoptichthys jordani
(Blind Cave Fish) Mexico, 8cm (73)

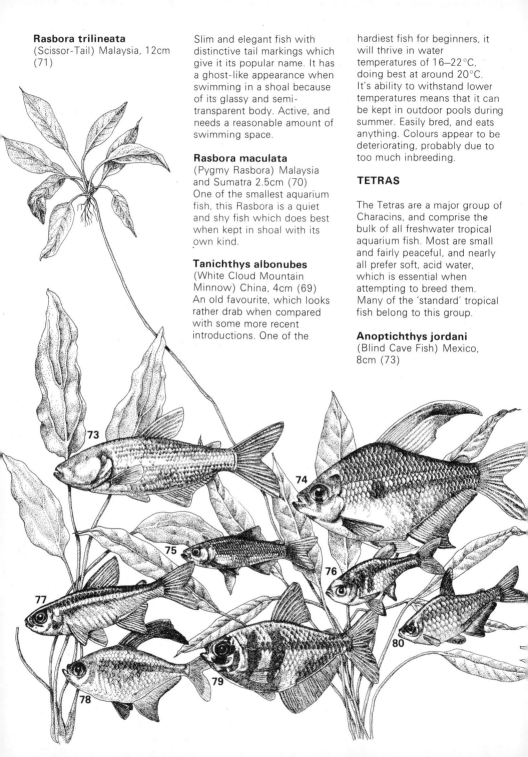

This pearl-coloured fish has no eyes at all, living originally in caves, but adapting surprisingly well to aquarium life, and fending for itself even in the community tank. It possesses an eerie ability to find its way about, seldom if ever bumping into anything. Breeds easily and eats any food offered.

Aphyocharax rubripinnis

(Bloodfin) Argentina, 5cm (75)
Small schooling fish with brilliant red fins. Undemanding and relatively easy to breed. Needs plenty of swimming space.

Cheirodon axelrodi

(Cardinal Tetra) S. America, 4cm, (77)
The introduction of this spectacular fish in 1956 created something of a sensation, as it outclasses the more familiar Neon Tetra. Its belly is fiery red, while much of the back and sides are covered with iridescent turquoise blue. It prefers soft water, and although formerly difficult to breed, currently available stock breeds fairly readily. Hardier than the Neon Tetra, and not susceptible to *Plistophora*, the Neon Disease. Keep only in shoals, or the fish will be very shy.

Gymnocorymbus ternetzi

(Black Widow Tetra) S. America, 5.5cm (78)
Another old favourite, which is very handsome when in good condition. Younger fish are marked with a velvety black colouration on the rear of the body, which fades as the fish grows. Easily bred, and hardy.

Hemigrammus caudovittatus

(Buenos Aires Tetra) Argentina, 7cm (85)
Large and boisterous Tetra, rather prone to fin nipping and to biting pieces out of the plants.

Hemigrammus erythrozonus

(Glowlight Tetra) Guyana, 4.5cm (88)
One of the most popular Tetras, with a bright red line along the flanks. Not easy to breed, and demands soft acid water.

Hemigrammus ocellifer

(Beacon Fish, Head-and-Tail Light Tetra) Guyana, 4.5cm (86)
Named after iridescent patches on the flanks and head. Breeds easily, and is hardy when kept as a shoal.

Hemigrammus rhodostomus

(Red-Nosed Tetra) Brazil, 4cm (87)
Bright red head, and attractive black and white marking on the tail. Popular shoaling fish which is unfortunately very difficult to spawn.

Hyphessobrycon callistus

(Jewel Tetra) S. America, 4cm (81)
Delicately shaded in pink and red, with a distinctive black edge to the anal fin, dark dorsal, and dark shoulder blotch.

Hyphessobrycon flammeus

(Flame Tetra, Rio Tetra) Brazil, 4.5cm (76)
Small Tetra seen at its best only when in breeding condition, when the male is flushed with deep orange.

Hyphessobrycon griemi

(Griem's Tetra) Brazil, 3cm (79)
Very dainty and attractive Tetra resembling *H. flammeus*, but smaller. Seldom available.

Hyphessobrycon herbertaxelrodi

(Black Neon) S. America, 3.5cm (83)
Iridescent green back, with a velvety black longitudinal stripe. Very popular as a schooling fish, but rather difficult to breed and consequently not always available.

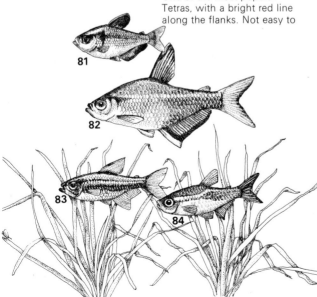

Hyphessobrycon pulchripinnis

(Lemon Tetra) S. America, 5cm (82)
More subtly coloured than many other Tetras, with a more ordinary body shape. Very prolific if it can be persuaded to breed.

Hyphessobrycon rosaceus

(Rosy Tetra) Guyana, 4cm (74)
A beautiful and scarce Tetra, which may be synonymous with *H. ornatus*. Males have elongated, sickle-shaped dorsal fins which develop with age. Difficult to breed, and most stock is imported and expensive. Can be rather delicate.

Hyphessobrycon serpae

(Serpae Tetra) S. America, 4.5cm (80)
Many sub-types exist, but all are orange or red throughout, with black marking on the fins. Breeds in typical fashion for a Tetra.

Megalamphodus megalopterus

(Black Phantom Tetra) S. America, 4.5cm (89)
Attractive Tetra resembling *Hyphessobrycon* species, and with marked diversity between males and females, female being red, while the male is grey.

Megalamphodus sweglesi

(Red Phantom Tetra) S. America, 4cm (91)
Recent introduction with overall red colouring, and a black shoulder spot. Hard to breed.

Moenkhausia oligolepis

(Glass Tetra) S. America, 12cm (92)
Hefty and tough Tetra, which is a fin-nipper. Best suited to communities with larger fish.

Moenkhausia pittieri

(Diamond Tetra) Venezuela, 6cm (90)
Iridescent silver all over. Easily bred and hardy, preferring soft water.

Nematobrycon palmeri

(Emperor Tetra) Colombia, 5.5cm (93)
Brown and iridescent blue, with a unique three-lobed tail in old males. Unlike other Tetras, does not shoal, but lives near the bottom showing territorial behaviour rather like a Cichlid. Difficult to breed and expensive.

Paracheirodon innesi (or *Hyphessobrycon innesi*)

(Neon Tetra) S. America, 4cm (84)
One of the classic aquarium Tetras, now quite cheap and easy to breed, although very susceptible to *Plistophora* infections. Less particular about water conditions than are some other Tetras.

Pristella riddlei

(X-ray Fish) S. America. 4.5cm (94)
Subtly coloured but attractive Tetra which needs plenty of swimming space. Thrives best in a large school, and can tolerate hard water.

Thayeria boehlkei

(Penguinfish) S. America, 6cm (95)
Hardy and familiar Tetra which 'hovers' in a tail-down attitude, but is capable of moving very fast. Best kept in a shoal. A fin-nipper, but worth keeping because of its unusual oblique marking, extending into the lower lobe of the caudal fin.

CHARACINS

Although Tetras are the commonest fish of the huge family of Characins to be kept in the home aquarium, they are by no means the only types suitable for the amateur.

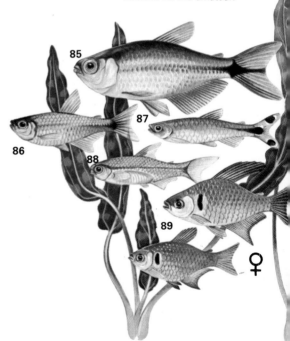

Indeed, some of the other Characins present more diverse shapes and oddities of behaviour than almost any other group of fish. Some are suitable only for the expert or the specialist; others are hardy and easy to keep. But like the Tetras, the remainder of the Characin group are very difficult to breed, having extraordinarily specialized water requirements during breeding, although living in normal tap water quite happily for most of the time.

Anostomus anostomus
(Striped Headstander)
Amazon and Guyana, up to 18cm (101)
A large handsome fish with broad longitudinal stripes and blood-red fins. The body is elongated and appears rigid, the fish swimming with only small movements of the tail. Chiefly remarkable for its tiny upturned mouth, which necessitates the fish turning into strange positions as it feeds. Omnivorous, and likes filamentous algae. A territorial fish, best kept singly, or with a large group of its own kind. May be a fin-nipper. Keep tank well covered, as it jumps.

Carnegiella strigata
(Marbled Hatchetfish)
S. America, 4.5cm (96)
Deep-bodied surface-feeder, capable of enormous leaps, using its pectoral fins as 'wings'. Very peaceful, and prefers soft acid water. Breeds rarely, in clumps of fine-leaved plants.

Chilodus punctatus
(Spotted Headstander)
S. America, 9cm (102)

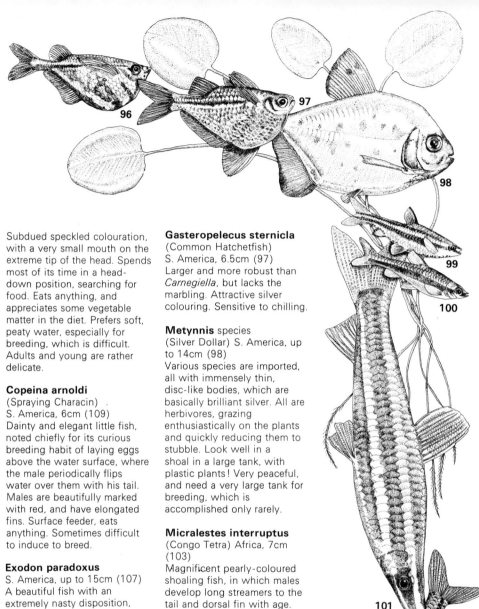

Subdued speckled colouration, with a very small mouth on the extreme tip of the head. Spends most of its time in a head-down position, searching for food. Eats anything, and appreciates some vegetable matter in the diet. Prefers soft, peaty water, especially for breeding, which is difficult. Adults and young are rather delicate.

Copeina arnoldi
(Spraying Characin) .
S. America, 6cm (109)
Dainty and elegant little fish, noted chiefly for its curious breeding habit of laying eggs above the water surface, where the male periodically flips water over them with his tail. Males are beautifully marked with red, and have elongated fins. Surface feeder, eats anything. Sometimes difficult to induce to breed.

Exodon paradoxus
S. America, up to 15cm (107)
A beautiful fish with an extremely nasty disposition, making it suitable only for the specialist. Can only be kept with its own kind. Colouring is iridescent silver with a violet sheen, and large black patches on shoulder and tail root. Carnivorous, and will attack much larger fish. Breeds rarely.

Gasteropelecus sternicla
(Common Hatchetfish)
S. America, 6.5cm (97)
Larger and more robust than *Carnegiella*, but lacks the marbling. Attractive silver colouring. Sensitive to chilling.

Metynnis species
(Silver Dollar) S. America, up to 14cm (98)
Various species are imported, all with immensely thin, disc-like bodies, which are basically brilliant silver. All are herbivores, grazing enthusiastically on the plants and quickly reducing them to stubble. Look well in a shoal in a large tank, with plastic plants! Very peaceful, and need a very large tank for breeding, which is accomplished only rarely.

Micralestes interruptus
(Congo Tetra) Africa, 7cm (103)
Magnificent pearly-coloured shoaling fish, in which males develop long streamers to the tail and dorsal fin with age. Only seen at its best in soft water and high temperatures. Peaceful but carnivorous. Difficult to breed.

Nannostomus aripiragensis
(Golden Pencilfish) Amazon, 4cm (100)

The most spectacular of a group of small Pencilfish, all very similar in shape and habit. They hold their bodies stiffly in the water, and eat only the smallest foods. The young are very difficult to raise, having very small mouths which make them hard to feed. Very peaceful, and suitable for the community tank, if the other fish are not too boisterous.

Nannostomus marginatus
(Dwarf Pencilfish) Surinam and Guyana, 3.5cm (99)
Smaller, daintier, but less colourful than the preceding species.

Poecilobrycon harrisoni
Guyana, 6cm (104)
Unusual Pencilfish which has seldom been bred. Colours are very distinct for a fish of this group.

Poecilobrycon trifasciatus
(Three-striped Pencilfish) S. America, 6cm (106)

Closely resembles *Nannostomus* species. Body is attractively striped and fins have blood-red blotches on their bases. Breeding is difficult.

Poecilobrycon unifasciatus
(One-lined Pencilfish) S. America, 6cm (105)
Similar to above, but with a single, better-defined longitudinal band.

Serrasalmus species
(Piranha) S. America, 35cm (108)
This and several related fish are extremely dangerous in their native waters. In the aquarium, the Piranha is a quiet and apparently inoffensive fish, resembling *Metynnis*, but is quite capable of biting a chunk clean out of the aquarist's hand. Treat with great respect, and keep singly to avoid cannibalism. Feed on worms, meat, and small fish. Difficult to raise to maturity.

LIVEBEARERS

Dermogenys pusillus
(Halfbeak) S.E. Asia, 7.5cm (111)
This little fish is unrelated to the true livebearers, even though it gives birth to live young. It resembles a tiny Swordfish, with its elongated lower jaw, and is a shy surface-living fish. Broods are very small and are difficult to rear. Prefers some salt in the water, and will eat only live foods and some floating foods with a high protein content. Tends to jump out of uncovered tanks.

Poecilia reticulata
(Guppy) S. America, introduced elsewhere, up to 5cm (115)
Little need be said about the famous Guppy, which breeds so easily and prolifically, females producing young every 4 weeks. It is available in an almost infinite range of

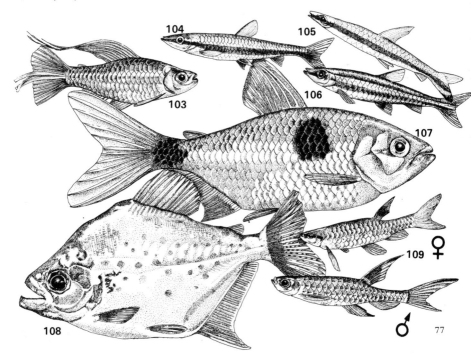

77

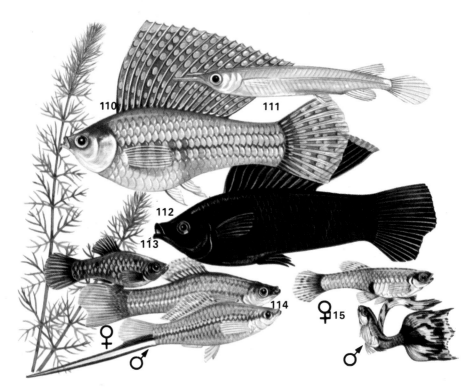

colours and fin shapes, all of which hybridize readily, and is the ideal aquarium fish for the beginner.

Poecilia sphenops
(Mollie) Central America, up to 12cm (112)
The standard aquarium Mollie, usually seen as a hybrid with another species of *Poecilia*. The true *P. spenops* does not have an enlarged dorsal fin, and the wild type is an insignificant green colour. Females are much larger than males. Demands a high level of vegetable matter in the diet. For breeding, use standard livebearer techniques, but add some salt to the water in the breeding tank. Avoid handling or disturbing heavily pregnant females.

Poecilia velifera
(Mexican Sailfin Mollie) Mexico, up to 15cm or more for imported wild fish, less in the aquarium (110)
The largest of the Mollies, with an enormous dorsal fin only in adult males. Tank-bred fish seldom have the enormous fins of the parent. Hardy, and breeds as other Mollies.

Xiphophorus helleri
(Swordtail) Central America, up to 12cm (114)
Originally green, the Swordtail now comes in a wide range of colourings, mostly hybridized with other *Xiphophorus* species. Males carry the spectacular sword on the tail. Sex changes are quite frequent in this fish. Breeds very readily.

Xiphophorus maculatus
(Platy) Central America, up to 12cm (113)
Very hardy indeed. One of the easiest of all fish to breed, and the fry are easy to rear, being so much larger than those of the Guppy.

KILLIFISH

Aphyosemion australe
(Lyretail) W. Africa, 5cm (119)
Fairly hardy and easily kept. An annual fish in nature, but in the aquarium eggs will hatch without drying out.

Aphyosemion bivittatum
W. Africa, 5cm (116)
Small, and peaceful enough for the community tank.

Aphyosemion gardneri
Nigeria and Cameroons, 6cm (118)

Predominantly green, with
yellow and red markings. Very
pugnacious. Variable in colour,
and may hybridize with other
species.

Aphyosemion sjoestedti
(Blue Gularis) Nigeria, 14cm
(117)
Largest of the group, the Blue
Gularis is very variably marked,
but predominantly iridescent
blue or green in colouration.
In males, the tail is drawn out
into thread-like streamers.
Males fight, so Blue Gularis is
best kept in pairs. Spawns on
the bottom, and eggs need
resting before they will hatch.

Aplocheilus dayi
(Ceylon Killie) India and Sri
Lanka, 10cm (121)
Similar to *A. lineatus* but
smaller and more to be trusted
in the community tank.

Aplocheilus lineatus
(Panchax lineatus) India and
Sri Lanka, 10cm (120)
Large and voracious fish. Very
hardy and exclusively
carnivorous. Lays eggs on
plants or spawning mop. Not
to be trusted with small fish.

Epiplatys annulatus
(Clown Killie, Rocket Panchax)
W. Africa, 4cm (122)
The most beautiful of the
group. Hardy, but difficult to
breed. Fry are especially
delicate.

Epiplatys dageti monroviae
(Firemouth Epiplatys) Liberia,
6cm (123)
Formerly known as *Panchax
chaperi*, this fish is small,
hardy and peaceful, and males
have a brilliant red throat.

LABYRINTH FISH

Betta splendens
(Siamese Fighting Fish)
Malaysia and Thailand, 6cm (124)

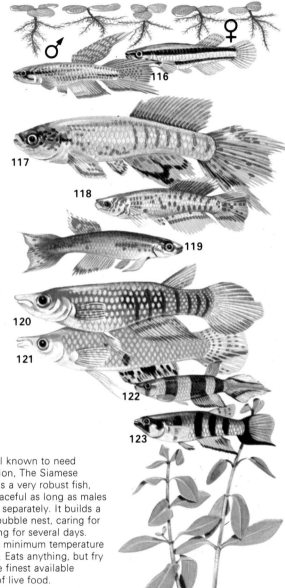

Too well known to need
description, The Siamese
Fighter is a very robust fish,
fairly peaceful as long as males
are kept separately. It builds a
typical bubble nest, caring for
the young for several days.
Needs a minimum temperature
of 25°C. Eats anything, but fry
need the finest available
grades of live food.

Colisa chuna
(Honeycomb Gourami) India,
7cm (125)
Hardy and easily bred bubble-
nester, although tank-raised
fish are less colourful than
wild imports.

Colisa fasciata
(Giant Gourami) India and
Burma, 12cm (132)
Like a larger, more aggressive,
and less colourful *C. lalia*. Care
and breeding as for any other
Gourami.

Colisa lalia
(Dwarf Gourami) India, 5cm
(126)
Small and brightly coloured,
and breeds readily in a
well-planted tank. Beware that
the male does not kill the
female after mating.

Macropodus opercularis
(Paradise Fish) China, 9cm
(131)
Magnificent but aggressive fish
which breeds readily at
ordinary room temperatures.
Extremely hardy, but not to be
trusted with shyer fish.

**Sphaerichthys
osphromenoides**
(Chocolate Gourami)
Malaysia and Sumatra, 6cm
(127)
Beautiful but delicate
Gourami, which appears to
incubate eggs in the mouth.
Very sensitive to disease;
requires soft acid water for
breeding, and high
temperatures.

Trichogaster leeri
(Pearl Gourami) S.E. Asia,
11cm (128)
Magnificently coloured,
especially when breeding.
Hardy and prolific.

Trichogaster trichopterus
(Three-spot Gourami) S.E.
Asia, 15cm (130)
Largely replaced by
T. trichopterus sumatranus
(129) the Blue Gourami, a
very hardy and aggressive fish,
suitable for communities with
larger fish only.

MISCELLANEOUS FISH

Brachygobius xanthozona
(Bumblebee Fish) Indonesia,
4.5cm (134)

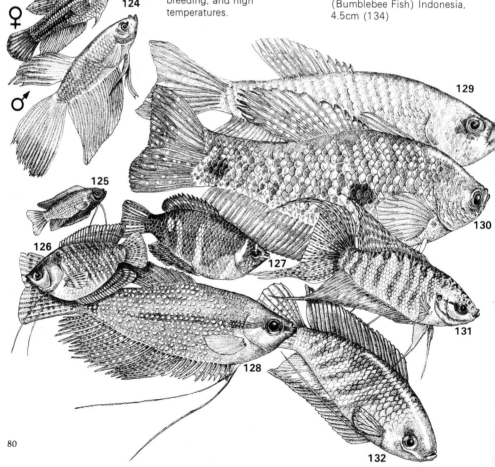

124

♀

♂

125

126

127

128

129

130

131

132

Tiny but bold Goby which can look after itself even with larger tankmates. Appreciates some salt in the water. Breeds like the Dwarf Cichlids.

Carinotetraodon somphongsi
(Thai Puffer) Thailand, 7.5cm (137)
Attractive and peaceful freshwater Puffer, guaranteed to rid your tank of all snails. Male has bright red and blue fins. Territorial with its own

kind, otherwise safe with all but the smallest fish.

Chanda ranga
(Indian Glassfish) India and S.E. Asia, up to 7cm (141)
Transparent and delicately marked fish which appreciates some salt in the water. Eats only live food, breeds easily but young difficult to rear due to problem in obtaining living food of the right size.

Gnathonemus petersi
(Elephant Nose) W. Africa, 20cm (135)
Black fish with a curious barbel on the chin, with which it grubs out Tubifex from the gravel. Shy, and needs plenty of shelter.

Gnathonemus schilthuisi
(136)
Close relative of the Elephant Nose with a bulldog-like jaw. Quiet but easily tamed and will learn to feed from the hand.

Melanotaenia maccullochi
(Dwarf Rainbowfish) Australia, 7.5cm (140)
Active shoaling fish which is very hardy and easy to breed, laying its eggs among plants. Appreciates some salt.

Telmatherina ladigesi
(Celebes Sailfish) Celebes 7.5cm (138)
Pearly-coloured shoaling fish with long streamers on the dorsal and anal fins of males. Difficult to breed, and needs considerable swimming space.

Tetraodon palembangensis
S.E. Asia, 25cm (139)
Tough and aggressive freshwater Puffer, not to be trusted with other fish.

Xenomystus nigri
(Knifefish) W. Africa, 22cm (133)
Graceful, peaceful and rather retiring fish. Will not bother fish too large to gulp.

Fresh-water plants

Acorus gramineus (5)
Reed-like plant, 30cm, growing slowly from a creeping rhizome. Deteriorates slowly when grown submerged.

Anubias nana (2)
Slow-growing marsh plant, 20cm, prefers soft water and moderate light.

Aponogeton ulvaceus (1)
Large (35cm) light green plant growing from a corm. Ideal as a specimen, but prone to attack by herbivorous fish and snails.

Bacopa monniera (3)
Slow-growing and tough marsh plant, easily propagated by cuttings.

Cabomba species (4)
Fast-growing plant, needing plenty of light, otherwise becoming very stringy.

Ceratopteris thalictroides (6)
True aquatic fern, easily propagated, and fast-growing. Leaf shape very varied. Spreads by daughter plantlets.

Cryptocoryne species (7)
Many and varied types available. All need subdued light, soft acid water. Slow-growing and very decorative. Species available vary from 5cm to 40cm in height. Some types have purplish leaves. Most appreciate peat beneath the gravel, or can be grown in a pot containing compost.

Echinodorus amazonicus (9)
Amazon Swordplant, growing rapidly to at least 30cm. Tough and long-lived centre-piece for the tank.

Echinodorus radicans (10)
Similar to the above, with more heart-shaped leaves. Needs soft water and adequate light.

Echinodorus tenellus (8)
Dwarf Swordplant, 8cm, which spreads rapidly by runners. Ideal foreground plant.

Eleocharis acicularis (14)
Hairgrass, grows to 20cm in bright light, and is an ideal delicate foreground plant.

Elodea densa (13)
Fast-growing bunch plant which propagates easily from cuttings. Suitable for tropical or cold-water tanks.

Limnobium stoloniferum (11)
Floating plant which provides useful shade when required.

Limnophila indica (16)
Similar bunch plant with very pale crisp leaves, needing plenty of light, and preferring soft water.

Ludwigia natans (17)
Attractive reddish tinged leaves, but gradually deteriorates at the high temperatures in the tropical tank.

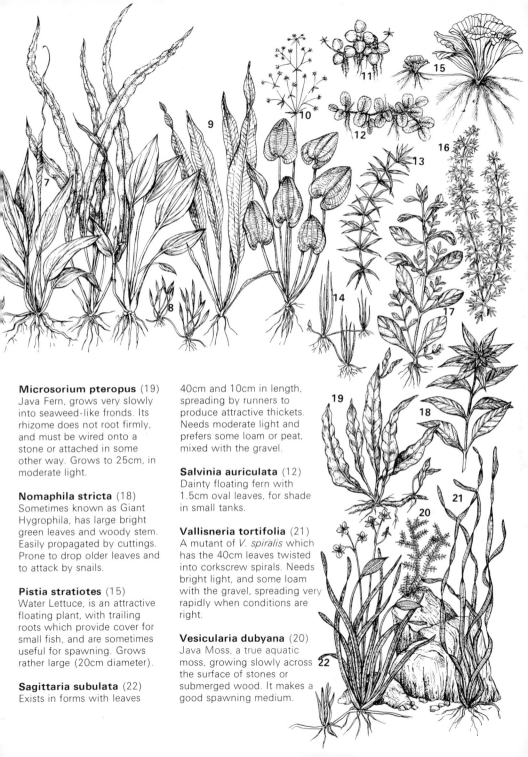

Microsorium pteropus (19)
Java Fern, grows very slowly into seaweed-like fronds. Its rhizome does not root firmly, and must be wired onto a stone or attached in some other way. Grows to 25cm, in moderate light.

Nomaphila stricta (18)
Sometimes known as Giant Hygrophila, has large bright green leaves and woody stem. Easily propagated by cuttings. Prone to drop older leaves and to attack by snails.

Pistia stratiotes (15)
Water Lettuce, is an attractive floating plant, with trailing roots which provide cover for small fish, and are sometimes useful for spawning. Grows rather large (20cm diameter).

Sagittaria subulata (22)
Exists in forms with leaves 40cm and 10cm in length, spreading by runners to produce attractive thickets. Needs moderate light and prefers some loam or peat, mixed with the gravel.

Salvinia auriculata (12)
Dainty floating fern with 1.5cm oval leaves, for shade in small tanks.

Vallisneria tortifolia (21)
A mutant of *V. spiralis* which has the 40cm leaves twisted into corkscrew spirals. Needs bright light, and some loam with the gravel, spreading very rapidly when conditions are right.

Vesicularia dubyana (20)
Java Moss, a true aquatic moss, growing slowly across the surface of stones or submerged wood. It makes a good spawning medium.

Guide to marine fish

1

2

Amphiprion ephippium
(Tomato Clownfish) Indo-Pacific, 15cm (7)
The hardiest and most satisfactory of the Clownfish. Frequently bred but young not often raised.

Amphiprion percula
(Clownfish) Indo-Pacific, 7cm (3)
The commonest Clownfish, can be kept successfully without its anemone home. Needs coaxing to start feeding, then will eat most dried foods. Quite hardy once established.

Centropyge fischeri
(Purple Fireball) Indo-Pacific, 7.5cm (12)
One of the few marine Angelfish which can be recommended for the home aquarium, keeping within a reasonable size. Brilliantly coloured and quite hardy, but very aggressive with its own kind. Usually expensive.

Chaetodon kleini
(Sunburst Butterflyfish) Indo-Pacific, 24cm (5)
Very unusual among Butterflyfish in being hardy and resistant to disease. Feeds well in captivity. Highly recommended.

Chromileptis altivelis
(Pantherfish) Indo-Pacific, up to 50cm (11)
Potentially enormous grouper, but seldom outgrows its tank. Keep only with fish large enough to be impossible to eat. Very tame, will feed from the hand. Hardy and long-lived. Ideal as a single specimen, or buy young and raise to full size in a very short time.

Dascyllus aruanus
(Humbug Damsel) Indo-Pacific, 8cm (1)
Cheap and tough Damsel, ideal for beginners, and for conditioning the gravel bed. Brightly coloured and bold, but very aggressive.

Dascyllus trimaculatus
(Domino) Indo-Pacific, 10cm (2)
Very tough and quarrelsome, best kept as a single specimen with other species.

Forcipiger longirostris
(Forceps Butterflyfish) Indo-Pacific, 20cm (6)
Has a reputation as a difficult fish, but quite hardy once established. Scavenges about in cracks in the coral with its long nose. Offer only fine foods, as its mouth is very small. Needs well-matured water.

Grammistes sexlineatus
(Six-lined Grouper) Indo-Pacific, 25cm (8)
Attractive but shy Grouper, which needs plenty of hiding places. Can produce poisonous black mucus from its anal gland when frightened, so try not to disturb the fish too much.

Heniochus acuminatus
(Pennant Coralfish) Indo-Pacific, 20cm (4)
Surprisingly robust although prone to damage of the long trailing dorsal fin. Eats anything, including flake and freeze-dried foods, and is hardy once established.

Labroides dimidiatus
(Cleaner Wrasse) Indo-Pacific, 10cm (10)
No tank should be without one of these cleaners, which remove parasites from the skin and gills of larger fish. They are not eaten, even by large predatory Groupers. Small, shy fish, which remain in hiding until larger fish come to be cleaned. Beware predatory false-cleaners, which resemble the real thing, but bite a piece out of their 'client'. These false-cleaners have an obvious undershot jaw, but are coloured like the true cleaner.

Thalassoma bifasciatum
(Bluehead) Caribbean and Atlantic, 25cm (9)
Attractive and hardy Wrasse which swims using only the pectoral fins. The young are yellow, and act as cleaners.

Dives under the gravel when frightened and at night. Hardy and peaceful; eats anything.

Acanthurus leucosternon
(White-breasted Surgeonfish) Indian Ocean, 30cm (20) Rather a delicate herbivorous Surgeonfish, best left to the more experienced aquarist. Very expensive and subject to shock when transferred to a new tank.

Canthigaster valentini
(Sharp-nosed Puffer), Indo-Pacific, 20cm (14) Very active and enquiring, and quite peaceful. Has odd habit of blowing sand away with jets of water to expose possible food.

Lactoria gibbosus
(Cowfish) Indo-Pacific up to 50cm, usually much smaller (16) Similar to *Tetrasomus*, with long cowlike horns. Rather prone to skin infections.

Pterois volitans
(Lionfish, Dragonfish) Indo-Pacific, up to 35cm (17) This fish and its relatives, although potentially large are inactive and can be kept in an ordinary tank—provided no small fish are present. Easily tamed, but beware the highly poisonous spines. Hardy and long-lived. Recommended.

Siganus lupinus (or Lo vulpinus)
(Foxface, Rabbitfish) Indo-Pacific, up to 25cm (15) Quiet and hardy fish. Eats anything. Beware poisonous spine in the dorsal fin. Aggressive only with its own kind.

Tetrasomus gibbosus
(Thornback Boxfish) Indo-Pacific, 30cm (13) Dull coloured, but with a strange geometric shell. Hardy and peaceful, eating almost anything.

Zebrasoma flavescens
(Yellow Tang) Hawaii, 30cm, (19)

Similar to *Z. veliferum*, but more peaceful, although not to be trusted with its own species or with other Tangs.

Zebrasoma veliferum
(Sailfin Tang) Indo-Pacific, 30cm (18)
Very active and handsome Tang, needing a considerable amount of swimming space. Keep individually, and try to obtain well acclimatized stock.

BRACKISH-WATER FISH

Monodactylus argenteus
(Malay Angel, Mono) Indo-Pacific, 20cm (23)
Like the following species, can live in varied salinities, and as an adult, needs marine conditions. Very active shoaling fish, needing plenty of space. Eats almost any-thing, and will nip pieces out of plant leaves. Recommended for brackish or marine tanks.

Scatophagus argus
(Scat) Indo-Pacific, estuarine and marine, up to 30cm (22)
Very tough scavenging fish, eating anything. Can live in totally fresh, brackish, or fully marine conditions, and can be acclimatized as required to differing salinities—but alter salinity slowly. An ideal fish for conditioning a marine gravel-filter bed. Peaceful, but competes with the other fish for food. Susceptible to fatal form of fungus infection when kept in fresh water.

Tetraodon fluviatilis
(Green Puffer) Indo-Pacific, 18cm (24)
Robust and rather aggressive puffer, readily available and usually cheap. Generally hardy, except prone to fungal attack when kept in water with too-low salinity. Can be kept satisfactorily in marine conditions. Sometimes breeds in captivity. Not to be trusted with small or slow-moving fish.

Toxotes jaculator
(Archerfish) coasts from Red Sea to Australia, 18cm (21)
A very attractive fish in its own right, but usually kept for its habit of shooting drops of water at flies, which it hits with unerring accuracy. Like the previous fish discussed, can be kept in almost any water conditions. In absence of flies, will eat almost anything available. Provide adequate hiding places to avoid bullying.

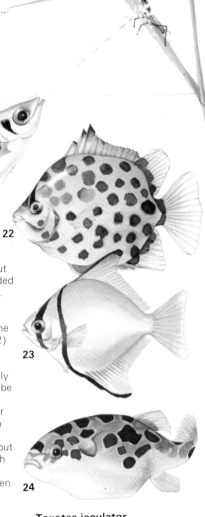

Book list

There are literally hundreds of reference books available on tropical fish, many of them expensive or highly technical. Those listed below contain information most useful for the beginner or the average enthusiast. Write to publishers for lists of their more specialized works.

Tropical Freshwater Aquaria, G. Cust and P. Bird, Hamlyn, 1970, 75p.
Small but comprehensive paperback with much valuable information and background on most of the common species.

Tropical Marine Aquaria, G. F. Cox, Hamlyn, 1971, 75p.
Companion volume to the above. It contains much sensible, practical information, and details of a good range of standard marine fish.

The Complete Home Aquarium, H. J. Mayland, Ward Lock, 1976, £4.95.
Compendious survey of both freshwater and marine aquaria. Like many other works translated from the German, this book examines the biology of the aquarium. Highly recommended.

Marine Tropical Fish in Colour, B. Walker, Blandford, 1975, £1.95.
Comprehensive pocket book with excellent photography. Very useful for identifying that obscure fish in the dealer's tank.

Collins Guide to Aquarium Fishes and Plants, A. Schiotz and P. Dahlstrom, Collins, 1972, £3.95.
Beautifully illustrated guide with brief details of most species of freshwater fish and the more common marine types. Useful general aquarist's manual.

Dr. Sterba's Aquarium Handbook, G. Sterba. Pet Library, 1973.
Very comprehensive A-Z of freshwater fish with full zoological details on identification and classification. A 'Bible' for the aquarist, but an even more comprehensive two-volume handbook by the same author is also available for the real enthusiast.

Aquarium Care, G. Sterba, Studio Vista, 1967.
Companion to the above, with details of plants, feeding, disease and hygiene. A little out-of-date but still very comprehensive and valuable.

Salt-water Tropical Fish in Your Home, G. Campbell, Sterling, 1976, £4.25.
Short but comprehensive work with interesting sections on diseases, breeding, and the maintenance of the fish.

Encyclopedia of Tropical Fishes, Dr Herbert Axelrod and William Vorderwinkler, TFH, £7.85.
A comprehensive aquarium classic on how to give fish the good care they need in order to breed successfully. It also covers the important aspects of aquarium maintenance.

Exotic Tropical Fishes
(Looseleaf Edition), TFH, £12.15.
An enormous reference volume covering all aspects of keeping tropical fish and plants. Its looseleaf format enables the reader to keep it up-to-date by inserting the supplement books published at eight-month intervals.

Exotic Marine Fishes
(Looseleaf Edition), TFH, £12.15.
Companion volume to the above giving a complete guide to the identification, keeping and breeding of marines. It is also kept up-to-date with regular supplements.

Illustrated Dictionary of Tropical Fish, Hans Frey, TFH, £6.05.
The only dictionary of tropical fish in the English language.

How to Keep and Breed Tropical Fishes, Dr Helmut Adler, TFH, £3.60.
A classic book in its field, with a good insight into the problems of the beginner.

Handbook of Tropical Aquarium Fishes, Dr Herbert Axelrod and Dr Leonard Schultz, TFH, £3.00.
Another enormous reference work, full of valuable information.

The above books published by TFH Publications are available from good booksellers and dealers, or direct from the publishers:
TFH (Great Britain) Ltd,
13 Nutley Lane,
Reigate, Surrey RH2 9HR.
To cover postage and packing add 47p for all orders up to £3.00, 55p for all orders up to £5.00, 85p for all orders up to £10.00, and £1.10 for orders of £10.00 and over.

Suppliers

Berkshire
The Goldfish Bowl
359 Oxford Road,
Reading
0734 582862

Buckinghamshire
Desborough Aquaria
32-3 Oxford Road,
High Wycombe
0494 35881

Clwyd
Rhyl Aquaria
2 Abbey Street,
Rhyl
0745 5595

Cornwall
Cornish Marine Aquatics
20 Pydar Street,
Truro
0872 77782

Cumbria
Carlisle Aquatics
55-7 Denton Street,
Denton Holme, Carlisle
0228 29700

Derbyshire
Matlock Waterlife Centre
Nottingham Road,
Tansley, Matlock
0865 62904

Devon
Devon Tropicals
150 Union Street,
Plymouth
0752 28158

Dorset
'Atlantis' Aquarium
466 Wimbourne Road,
Winton, Bournemouth
0202 53593

Durham
Grotto Aquaria
21 Frederick Street,
Sunderland
0783 59980

G. R. Metcalf
187 Northgate,
Darlington
0325 65991

Essex
Harlow Aquarium Supplies
Service Bay No. 6,
Staple Tye, Harlow
0279 20098

C. J. Skilton
Great Gibcracks Chase,
Butts Green, Sandon,
Chelmsford
0245 400535

Glamorgan
Blue Water Aquatics
16 Macintosh Place,
Cardiff
0222 21660

Gloucestershire
Everglades Aquatic Nurseries
Baunton,
Nr. Cirencester
0285 4656

Hampshire
Arundel Aviaries and Fisheries
313-5 Arundel Street,
Portsmouth
0705 20047

Wingate of Winchester
7 Market Street,
Winchester
0962 2406

London
Fins and Wings
Selfridges Ltd.
400 Oxford Street, W1
01-629 1234 extn. 698

Fairburns Aquaria Ltd
15 Well Hall Parade
Eltham, SE9
01-850 5859

Hendon Aquatics
19 Finchley Lane,
Hendon, NW4
01-203 4829

Pets Galore
45 Blackbird Hill,
Kingsbury, NW9
01-205 2230

Mayfair Aquarium and Pet Store
122 Upper Tooting Road,
SW17
01-672 7977

Tachbrook Tropicals Ltd
244 Vauxhall Bridge Road,
Victoria, SW1
01-834 5179

Monmouthshire
Top Trop Aquatics
123 Caerleon Road,
Newport, Gwent
0633 54496

Oxfordshire
The Goldfish Bowl
253 London Road,
Headington, Oxford
0865 62904

Suffolk
Exotarium
29-31 St Margaret's Street,
Ipswich
0473 212234

Yorkshire
Keith Barraclough Aquarist Ltd
Hayfield Mills,
Haycliffe Lane,
Bradford BD5 9ET
0274 76241

Northern Ireland
Grosvenor Tropicals
86-8 Woodstock Road,
Belfast BT6 8AE
0232 56246

Scotland
G.A.F.S. Tropical House,
4-5 Kirkwood Place,
Edinburgh
031-661 3520

Glossary

inland salt lakes, it has eggs which resist drying out. Easily cultured, suitable food for young fish. Adults available frozen or freeze-dried, for feeding larger fish.

Coral: stone growth produced by tiny marine animals resembling Anemones. Difficult to keep alive in the aquarium, but cleaned coral is very decorative in the marine tank. Don't use in freshwater tanks.

Crustaceans: small animals with jointed external skeletons, useful as food for aquarium fish, eg. Daphnia and Brine Shrimp.

Daphnia: small freshwater Crustacea, excellent live food, but have laxative action if given too frequently.

Egg-binding: relatively unusual disorder in which female fish become swollen with eggs which they are unable to discharge from their bodies.

Electric organs: Mormyrids or Elephant Noses navigate by means of weak electric fields. Electric Eels and Electric Catfish actually stun or kill their prey with more powerful discharges.

Fibre glass: to avoid corrosion, some marine tanks have frames built from fibre glass, which also provides some flexibility and added strength.

Filters: (see p. 35) Devices to remove small solid particles suspended in the aquarium water.

Flukes: parasitic worms, often present in wild-caught fish.

Adipose fin: small, fatty fin situated between dorsal fin and the tail. Found in some Catfish, Characins, and members of the Salmon family.

Aerator: device for forcing small air bubbles into the water, usually by passing air through porous stone or plastic.

Albino: fish lacking any skin colouring, and generally a natural pink, such as the Blind Cave Fish.

Algae: primitive plant, sometimes microscopic, or threadlike. Develops in excess light, and forms important part of diet for some fish.

Breeding mops: bunches of nylon wool or bunch plants into which certain species of fish scatter their eggs.

Breeding trap: device to keep fish away from their eggs or young, to prevent cannibalism. May be easily improvised, or bought ready-made in several types and sizes.

Brine shrimp (*Artemia salina*): small crustacean inhabiting

Very difficult to treat.

Fry: the young of any fish.

Gasping: convulsive gulping actions at the water surface in fish suffering from lack of oxygen. CO_2 build-up, or toxic water conditions.

Glass aquaria: modern tank without a metal frame, and therefore not prone to corrosion, nor to drying-out of mastic or putty.

Gonopodium: modified anal fin in a Livebearer, used to deposit sperms in the female.

Grouper: potentially very large, sedentary, and completely carnivorous marine fish.

Hardness: measure of the amount of dissolved minerals in the water. Usually caused by lime and magnesium salts.

Heaters: they usually consist of a heating coil protected by a hard glass tube, which can be safely submerged in the tank.

Hydra: anemone-like animal, capable of catching and eating very small fry.

Hydrometer: device to measure the amount of chemicals dissolved in the water. Usually used to determine the correct salinity when mixing artificial sea water.

Ich: general name for skin diseases causing fish to rub themselves on plants or rockwork.

Infusoria: microscopic animals used as food for smallest fry, cultured from decaying plant material.

Labyrinth organ: organ which acts as a 'lung', allowing labyrinth fish to breathe air from the water surface.

Leech: worm-like animal which may attach itself to fish and suck blood. Otherwise most unsightly.

Methylene Blue: very powerful but non-toxic blue dye, useful for treating many diseases of freshwater fish. May kill plants and stain gravel.

Mouthbrooders or

Mouthbreeders: fish which incubate eggs or rear young in their mouths.

Nauplii: the young of the Brine Shrimp.

Oxygen: gas essential to life which dissolves in the aquarium water.

Parasite: animal or fungus living internally or externally on another creature, and causing it harm in various ways eg. white spot, flukes, some leeches.

pH: a measure of the acidity or alkalinity of the water. May be critical when attempting to breed sensitive species.

Phantom Shrimps: aquatic fly larvae. Uncommon, but sometimes found with Daphnias. Excellent fish food.

Plants: those kept in the freshwater tank may be flowering plants, ferns, mosses, or algae. In the marine tank, some larger algae can be kept, with limited success.

Plastic aquarium: useful small tank for breeding or quarantine. Very easily scratched, so not generally suited for display purposes.

Polyp: individual animal in a coral colony. Preyed upon by some Butterflyfish.

Quarantine tank: small unfurnished tank for new acquisitions. Its use allows infection to become apparent before new fish are added to the main tank. Infected fish can usually be treated in the quarantine tank.

Rocks: used for decoration, but care must be taken that they are inert and will not release poisonous substances into the water.

Salinity: amount of salt dissolved in the water. Must be precisely measured in the marine tank.

Scavenger: fish or any other organism which feeds upon aquarium waste. eg. snails, some catfish, marine shrimps, etc.

Shock: condition often leading to disease or death, following on from some disturbance.

Snails: most unwelcome in most tanks as they feed on plant leaves, and breed quickly.

Swim bladder: organ which contains gas, and gives the fish its neutral buoyancy. Sometimes diseased, in which case fish float helplessly, or sink to the bottom.

Temperature: all tropical fish require control of the aquarium temperature, living healthily only within a narrow temperature range.

Thermometer: essential for the monitoring of water temperatures. Many modern types are now available.

Thermostat: device which switches heaters on and off to maintain approximately constant temperature.

Index

Credits

Artists
Pamela Dowson
RonHayward Art Group
Sally Launder
Pat Lenander
Vanessa Luff

Chris Perfect
John Shackell

Photographs
Heather Angel, 5, 27, 54
Paul Forrester, 37
Dr Guiseppe Mazza, 25, 26
Photo Aquatics/Jaroslav Elias,
    41
Mike St Maur Sheil, 44, 45

Equipment for photograph on
page 37 kindly loaned by Fins
and Wings Limited, Selfridges,
London W1.

Cover
Design: Barry Kemp
Photograph: Jane Burton/
Bruce Coleman Ltd